Contents

Foreword

This volume features a selection of articles originally published in, or updated from, the first eight issues of *Ullans: The Magazine for Ulster-Scots*, the magazine of the Ulster-Scots Language Society. To date, issues of the magazine have been available only in a few libraries in Northern Ireland and to members of the Language Society. Because we believe that much of its material has wider interest and appeal, an editorial committee of the Society has organized the present collection. It includes items under three broad headings: Ulster-Scots Culture (highlighting creative arts, sports, and other areas of traditional culture), Ulster-Scots Language (focusing on names, vocabulary and history), and Ulster-Scots Writing (prose, fiction, and poetry written in the language). The first two sections deal extensively with connections with Scotland.

The Ulster-Scots Language Society was established in 1992 to promote the study and use of Ulster Scots, one of the three traditional languages (along with Irish and English) of the historical province of Ulster. Since that time Ulster Scots has steadily gained public awareness across Northern Ireland and beyond. The Society has played an important role in stimulating new writing in Ulster Scots and in giving a voice to those wanting to express themselves in this language of their childhood and communities. Although most work featured here is of recent vintage, writing in Ulster Scots is hardly a new development. Thus, we have included items representing every stage of Ulster-Scots literature since the early seventeenth century, when thousands of Scots arrived, especially in the Plantation of Ulster, to settle in Antrim, Down, and elsewhere in Ulster. In many of those areas Ulster Scots has been spoken continuously for four centuries.

Ulster Scots is historically related to English. The two are similar in some ways, but in others are fundamentally different. One of these is that Ulster Scots presently lacks standard spelling. Those who write in it often rely on the spoken form of the language as a guide. In other words, they 'follow their ear' and do not conform to a single way of spelling even common words such as the following pronouns, prepositions and verbs:

English	Ulster Scots	English	Ulster Scots
I	*a, A, ah, I*	*of*	*o', o', of, uv*
they	*thae, thai, the, the', they*	*to*	*tae, ti, til, to*
was	*was, wes, wus, wuz*	*were*	*war, were, wur*
with	*wae, we, wi, wi', with*	*your*	*yer, ye'r, your*

The variations within written Ulster Scots may seem strange to the eye and even unpredictable, but they are generally based on pronunciation. Writers simply differ in how they believe specific sounds should be spelled. Ulster Scots is not for silent reading! Those who follow the simple practice of reading aloud will understand far more of it, even if they're not from Ulster. At the same time, many Ulster-Scots spellings (eg *tae, wi*) are traditional ones that have been employed for centuries to write Scots in Ulster or Scotland (eg the work of Robert Burns). One day Ulster Scots will almost certainly have a more uniform system of spelling, but at the present time it is variable. The magazine *Ullans* has actively encouraged writers to experiment, in the hope that in future accepted spelling will gradually and naturally develop.

In some selections in this book Ulster-Scots words are defined either in a glossary at the end or, in one case of poetry, alongside the text. It has proven impractical to add definitions of words to other articles. Readers who want to look up individual terms they find or to explore the vocabulary, grammar or history of Ulster Scots, should consult the following sources:

M Robinson et al (eds.), *Concise Scots Dictionary* (Aberdeen University Press, 1985)
C Macafee (ed.), *Concise Ulster Dictionary* (Oxford University Press, 1996)
P Robinson, *Ulster-Scots: A Grammar of the Traditional Written and Spoken Language* (Ullans Press, 1997)
J Fenton (ed.), *The Hamely Tongue: A Personal Record of Ulster-Scots in County Antrim* (Ullans Press, 2000)

We encourage readers to read written Ulster Scots aloud whenever possible, listen to it in the Ulster countryside, and develop their own ears for it. We sincerely hope that the publication of this collection will kindle greater use of Ulster Scots as both a spoken and a written medium.

Thanks to all the authors for permitting us to reprint their work in this anthology.

The Editors

Ulster Tartan

Ulster Tartan

by Leslie Dickson
ORIGINALLY PUBLISHED IN ULLANS NUMMER 3, SPRING 1995

Our cover design incorporates the colourful tartan that is the subject of this article.

Tartan. What does that word conjure up in your mind? Do you think of pipers marching to the skirl of their pipes with their kilts swinging? Or, do you recall a happy holiday spent in Scotland?

It will almost certainly be Scotland and the Scots which will come to mind, because the Scots have taken the tartan as their own and made it synonymous with their national identity.

Tartans are many and varied, and in 1963 the Lord Lyon King of Arms, who is responsible for all things heraldic, decided that as tartan has no true heraldic status, a body should be set up to register the authenticity of tartans. This was duly done and the body is called The Scottish Tartan Society, which operates from offices in Comrie in Perthshire. They have been given the remit of registering, recording and accrediting tartans and also enabling members of the public to trace claim to tartans and even design and register new tartans.

In Northern Ireland in 1956 an interesting event occurred in a lane leading to the farm of a Mr William Dixon just north of Dungiven in County Londonderry. A labourer working in the lane found some old clothing buried in the ditch. The garments consisted of a large semicircular woollen cloak, a woollen jacket and the remains of a pair of tartan trews that by their condition had obviously been buried for a very long time.

It is the pair of trews which is of interest to this author.

The articles of clothing were taken to the Ulster Museum in Belfast, where they were subjected to an intensive examination by a Miss Audrey Henshall; the details of her findings are fully recorded in a 23-page paper in the *Ulster Journal of Archaeology* in 1961/62. Because of the style of the jacket and features of the clothing in comparison with other writings and drawings, Miss Henshall dated them as probably being worn in the early to mid 1600s. She suggested that the cloak was Irish while the trews were almost certainly of Highland origin and would have been worn by someone of rank. Due to the type of soil, a peaty loam in which the clothing had lain buried for so long, the original colours were mainly stained to various shades of brown, so they were difficult to distinguish. However, four colours were identified, and Miss Henshall gave a clear description of what the cloth was probably like, including a diagrammatic picture of the tartan weave:

The cloth has a check pattern, the colours now being mainly
stained to various shades of brown so that they are difficult
to distinguish. Where best preserved it can be seen that four
colours have been used, probably red, dull green, dark brown
and orange or yellow. The ground consists of wide blocks of
red and green, divided into squares of about 1 ins., by groups
of narrow lines of dark orange, dark brown and green.

(Audrey S Henshall and Wilfred A Seaby, 'The Dungiven Costume', p.125)

As a follow-up to this find, a project was undertaken by various staff members of
the Ulster Museum to reproduce the garments. The tartan material was woven on a
hand-loom in the Belfast College of Technology, and the Museum staff dressed a model
in replica clothing. This model stood in the entrance hall of the Ulster Museum as an
introduction to their Elizabethan Ulster Exhibition in November 1958.

The model no longer exists, but the original and the reproduced clothing are stored
in the Ulster Museum and may be seen on request. The tartan cloth was reproduced in
two shades of brown with a red overcheck, and it is this design which was registered
with The Scottish Tartan Society in the early 1970s as the Ulster Tartan. The design has
been manufactured and sold under this name since.

Recently the colours which Miss Henshall described in her article have been woven
into a tartan material which is also manufactured. It too has been registered with the
Scottish Tartan Society as 'Ulster Tartan', bearing the same name and giving both
tartans authenticity.

This lays the ground for an interesting cross-reference between the Province and
Scottish culture. It is also of interest to note that this more recent Ulster Tartan, in red
and green with a yellow bounded with black overcheck, which more closely accords
with Miss Henshall's original description of the Ulster Tartan, is used as the tartan for
the kilts and uniform of the Dragoon Guards.

So Ulster has its own tartans which have been duly recorded and registered
as authentic. How about starting to wear them with pride and incorporating them
into our culture?

Jackie Stewart, Jamie Boyd and Friends:

Subscribers to Ulster-Scots Poetry 1793-1824: A Name Survey

by Ronnie R Adams

ORIGINALLY PUBLISHED IN ULLANS NUMMER 1, SPRING 1993

It was a common practice in the late 1700s and early 1800s for authors, especially those without enough capital to pay the printers or unable to gauge demand, to collect money (or at least a promise to buy) in advance from prospective purchasers. In return, the list of those who had subscribed was often printed in the book. In Ulster, such lists survive in eleven little books of poetry published by country rhymers, all containing some Ulster-Scots, ranging from, at one end of Ulster, Hugh Porter of Moneyslane and Andrew M'Kenzie of Dunover, in County Down, to David Colhoun, 'the Shepherd of Mary Grey', in County Tyrone. All eleven were published between 1793 and 1824. Between them the books contain a total of nearly 7,000 names, and from them can be extracted the most common surnames and forenames in the Ulster-Scots areas of Ulster at this time.

As might be expected, there was a vast array of surnames, but the most common, with more than fifty occurrences each, are listed below.

> Stewart/Stuart 97; Boyd 79; Thompson/Thomson 79; Moore 72;
> Wilson 67; Campbell 65; Hamilton 60; Johnston/Johnson 60;
> Brown 53; Smith/Smyth 53; Orr 51

Those with more than thirty occurrences are:

> Hunter 45; Ferguson/Fergusson 44; Bell 43; Patterson 39;
> M'Kee/M'Key/Makee 36; Allen/Allan/Alen 34; White/Whyte
> 34; Wallace 32; Robinson/Robison 32; Montgomery 31; Scott
> 31; Alexander 30

There was a large number of names with more than twenty occurrences. These are listed in alphabetical order below:

> Adams; Anderson; Caldwell/Callwell; Clark/Clarke;
> Craig/Craige; Crawford; Cunningham; Davidson/Davison;
> Finlay/Finley; Hill; Jameson/Jamison; Kelly; Kennedy; Kerr;

Kilpatrick/Kirkpatrick; Lowry; M'Connell; M'Cormick;
M'Cullough/M'Culloch; M'Dowell; McMullen/McMullan;
Martin; Maxwell; Miller; Neilson/Nelson; Rea/Ray; Reid/Read;
Shaw; Simpson; Young

There was a much smaller variety of forenames, and a large proportion of the population bore a relatively small number of them: for instance, nearly one male in four was called John. The top seventeen, that is, all forenames to score higher than 1% of the total, are listed below. The total number of forenames is less than the 7,000 surnames recovered, as many individuals were listed by initials only.

John 870; James 578; William 504; Robert 289; Thomas 205;
Samuel 156; Surnames as Forenames 120; Hugh 119; George 90;
Alexander 82; David 69; Andrew 69; Joseph 55; Charles 51;
Henry 51; Edward 50; Francis 38

A much smaller number of female forenames was recovered, as most of the over 700 women listed were known simply as Miss or Mrs. Just over one hundred female names occurred, and the list of those scoring higher than 1% includes:

Jane 20; Mary 18; Margaret 13; Ann/Anne 13; Eliza 8; Elizabeth
5; Isabella 5; Ellen 3; Sarah 2; Betty 2; Agnes 2

Much more work needs to be done on these names. For instance, they are almost invariably referenced to a townland or town, and even a preliminary examination reveals that the readership of these volumes closely corresponds with the Ulster-Scots speaking areas of Antrim, Down, and the Foyle basin. It is quite possible that this list of subscribers will prove to be the nearest thing obtainable to a past census of Ulster-Scots.

The 1956 World Championships, held at Balmoral Showgrounds

Pipe Bands

by Tommy Millar
ORIGINALLY PUBLISHED IN ULLANS NUMMER 1, SPRING 1993

T he 1992 Grade I World Championship, held in Bellahouston Park, Glasgow, was won by an Ulster band – Field Marshal Montgomery – with the two other prizes in the magical 'big six' leaderboard going to Australia and Canada respectively.[1] Of the 175 bands entered in the six grades of competition, one-third were from outside Scotland, endorsing the assertion that solo piping, which has been cosmopolitan for many years now, and pipe banding are truly international. From the perspective of the Province, which is the focus of this article, pipe band competition had its 'birth' prior to the outbreak of World War I, although the first record we have comes from around the early 20s, when all bands were under the umbrella of the North of Ireland Bands Association (NIBA). This body's competitions were usually confined to two each year, the principal one being held prior to Christmas, usually in the Ulster Hall or Grosvenor Hall in Belfast.

The piping fraternity was accommodated within this framework, although it did form what was termed the Northern Ireland Pipe Band League, which gave the members a little autonomy, while still operating in membership of the NIBA. World War II called a halt to all such activities, but on the cessation of hostilities in 1945, the League was re-formed at a meeting in Waring Street, Belfast, attended by six bands. It was decided to call another meeting, in September of that year, at which nine bands attended, namely Annahilt, Upper Crossgar, Ballycoan, Sydenham, Dromara, East Belfast, M'Quiston Memorial, Ballynahinch and Drumlough. Priority was given to the election of officers and the recruitment of more bands into membership. The chairman was David Nelson, senior, vice-chairman Eddie McVeigh, secretary Tom Hart, treasurer Norman Bradley, and the meetings were to be convened on the last Thursday of each month.

But there was still one little 'hiccup'. Pipe bands in the Province were still in membership of the NIBA, with Davy Nelson and Tommy Hart as the League's representatives. The only highlight, as stated earlier, was the series of annual contests in the Ulster Hall, usually spread over a week. Needless to say, it was standing room only on Saturday nights, this evening being allocated to the tartan travellers, with the rest of the evenings sparsely attended. But the 'natives' were getting restless, and during 1949 feelers were being sent to Glasgow with the intention of clearing the way for League bands to apply for membership of the then Scottish Pipe Band Association. The situation with regard to the NIBA was becoming untenable. It was a case of the tail wagging the dog, with the pipe bands attracting the largest crowds, yet being allocated a paltry one-night stand! Mr William Whitelaw (no connection of a former government official here), who was secretary of the SPBA during this period, answered the request for Association membership by intimating that if the Northern Ireland applicants could muster 10 bands, then a Branch could be 'raised' in the Province.

In the fullness of time (1950 to be exact) this was achieved, and a number of bands were the pioneers in what Edward McVeigh, MBE, JP, often proudly describes as the 'best day's business ever done' with regard to the propagation of piping and drumming in Northern Ireland. Ballynahinch, Ballycoan, Sydenham, Waringsford, St Joseph's, 8th Belfast Memorial, Duke of York, Raffrey, Boardmills and Rasharkin were the first intake. The city of Belfast and its environs alone at one time had 50 bands, although they were not all Association members. Yet today as a result of urban development, the Troubles, etc, only one band emanates from the city. The tartan scenario has moved almost completely to the country!

With the advent of the new Northern Ireland Branch, drumming classes were held right away, under a big name in Scottish percussion in those days – Drum Major Alec M'Cormick – with the result that 29 participants received certificates in the first examination taken by Northern Ireland Branch pupils. Piping instruction was not neglected in the formative years of the fledgling movement here. Pipe Major Donald MacLean spent some time in the Province instructing the pipe majors of the initial intake of member bands. Progress in building membership was fast and spontaneous, and the growth, enthusiasm and administrative capability was rewarded by the parent body in Glasgow. The 'mandarins' of Washington Street designated a major championship outside Auld Scotia for the first time in the Association's history – the European event held in Balmoral Showgrounds, Belfast, in 1953.

If there were any doubts or inhibitions on the part of the hierarchy in Glasgow as to whether its newest member branch could stand on its own feet, these were finally dispelled after the 'European', and the administrators in Ulster never looked back after that red-letter day! As a mark of the respect and confidence which the new branch had at headquarters, the Association designated two even bigger honours for its newest and fastest-growing branch: the 1956 and 1962 World Championships, also held at the spacious Balmoral Showgrounds. Since those formative years, Northern Ireland bands have travelled to the mainland, notably for the World's and Cowal Games events, and were not long in making their presence felt in the lower grades. In 1970, the now-defunct Robert Armstrong Memorial Band, under the late, lamented Tommy Geddis, won the Grade 2 World Championship at Aberdeen and were subsequently elevated to the big league (Grade 1) along with St Patrick's from Donaghmore in County Tyrone, led by Scot Tommy Anderson. This band, sadly, is also no longer with us.

As the standard improved, in later years the RAMs and St Pat's were joined by Cullybackey (which was the first Ulster band to make the play-offs in the old-style Grade 1 format), McNeillstown, Graham Memorial, RUC, Upper Crossgar, Field Marshal Montgomery and, most recently, Eden from near Omagh. Always there or thereabouts in the ever-increasing exodus to the five major events on the mainland, the Ulster bands finally achieved domination, as all true Ulster-Scots well know, in practically all the 'big ones' in August 1992. Yes, the centre of global pipe banding was, unbelievably, Ulster, with the Field Marshal Montgomery completely monopolising the scene – Scottish, British, Cowal, World, runner-up in the European – and culminating with the title of Supreme Champion of Champions. They were ably supported with high placings by the large contingent of Ulster bands over the other grades. Northern Ireland is now the largest branch in the Royal Scottish Pipe Band Association, with over ninety bands.

The province's drum majors have always set a parallel standard to that of the bands, with both world senior and juvenile titles returning more than once across the Channel. The dramatic progress in the raising of the musical standard at all levels in recent years can be attributed, in no small measure, to the activity of the Northern Ireland Branch's Education Committee, formed in the early 1980s, which was incorporated into the Piping and Drumming School in 1986. The distribution of certificates at the annual graduation each spring increases numerically and is an endorsement of the proficiency of the programme devised and executed by Principal Sam Bailie and his superb team of instructors, which includes such luminaries as Richard and Gordon Parkes, who have taken the Field Marshal Montgomery to such success.

Down the years, the Northern Ireland Branch, in its continual process of laying even firmer foundations and the subsequent raising of standards, has utilised the rich vein of resource available in the 'land of our forefathers'. Influential personalities have been invited to come 'o'er the water' and assist in this development, household names like Willie Sloan, A D Hamilton, Alec Duthart, Donald Macintosh, Alec M'Cormick, Tom MacAllister and his son, John K MacAllister, and many more. The last-mentioned duo – the MacAllister Connection – has made an important and vital contribution to progress in banding in this passionate piping Province, especially in the formative years.

And it is worth noting that the Branch has also supplied officials for the parent body, which received the 'Royal' prefix in 1980, during its four decades of membership. Edward McVeigh, who was honoured some years ago with the MBE by Her Majesty the Queen, was Association chairman six years and vice-chairman for three. Alistair Gray held the chair for one term, while Archie M'Kinley, one of the foundation officials of the branch here, was the Association treasurer for a period. Two Northern Ireland members now hold top positions in the Royal Scottish Pipe Band Association: President Tom M'Carroll, and Chairman George Ussher. In spite of the political and social upheaval of the recent past, the propagation of the music of the Noble Instrument has continued to progress – a strident affirmation of the character, resolution and determination of those of us proud to be called Ulster-Scots!

[1] Northern Ireland bands won the top two grades in the 2002 World Championships: Grade 1 was won by the Field Marshal Montgomery Band, based in Carryduff, County Down, and Ballycoan won Grade 2.

Ulster-Scots Country Dancing, early 1970s

Scottish Country Dancing

by Elma Wickens
ORIGINALLY PUBLISHED IN ULLANS NUMMER 1, SPRING 1993

There is little doubt that in Scotland dancing is in the blood and that the Scot does not leave his native dances behind him when travelling overseas. It was probably in the fourteenth century that dancing in sets of eight or more people originated in Scotland, but reference to it is scant until the 1600s. French influence at the time of Mary Queen of Scots is often mentioned as a possibility. The popularity of fiddling and dancing grew together in the late 1700s, and in the early nineteenth century another new dancing craze swept through the British Isles. This was the Quadrille, which had been introduced from France about 1815, and quickly a whole range of square dance quadrilles became popular, such as the Lancers, the Waltz Cotillion, the Caledonians, and the D'Albert. The Scots absorbed some of the new square dances into their own mode of dancing, such as the ever-popular Round Reel of Eight. In turn, dances like the Caledonians developed in the nineteenth century as forms of rural square dances in North America, Scotland and Ulster, set largely to Scottish traditional tunes and influenced by the older traditions of Scottish dancing. Professional dancing teachers have existed throughout Scotland since at least about 1771. One of the best-known was Scott Skinner, active in the late nineteenth and early twentieth centuries, who taught in the north-east of Scotland before he achieved fame as a fiddler.

In the days before the advent of the cassette tape and compact disk, live music was of course an essential element in the enjoyment of an evening's dancing:

> Hey! for the music o' Baldy Bain's fiddle!
> Redd up the barn, an' we'll gie ye a reel.
> In till it, too! wi' a diddle-dum-diddle.
> Dod! that's the tune to put springs in your heel.
> From 'The Barn Dance' by W D Cock

Country dancing had declined by the time of the First World War, and the traditional fiddlers were a dying race. Then almost eighty years ago a group of people interested in Scottish Country Dances met in Glasgow. The meeting, called by Mrs Ysobel Stewart of Fasnacloich and Miss Jean Milligan of Glasgow on 26 November 1923, marked the beginning of the movement, which is now world-wide, known as the Royal Scottish Country Dance Society. Such was the interest in Scotland and elsewhere that there are now over 28,000 members in over 150 branches, as well as dancers in over 500 affiliated groups throughout the world.

In Northern Ireland there are three Branches of the Society, one in Belfast, one in Portrush and one in Whitehead. The Belfast Branch was formed in 1946 and now has a membership of almost 300, who attend eight weekly classes. Three of the classes are held in Belfast (in the Lisburn Road, Malone Road and Castlereagh Road areas), two in Bangor, one in Helen's Bay, one in Lisburn and one in Whitehouse. In addition, an affiliated class operates in Comber, and an independent one in Ballylesson. For those just starting to enjoy country dancing, the Belfast Branch periodically runs a Beginners' Class. In the Belfast area, it is therefore possible to dance every night of the week except Sunday!

Scottish dancing is suitable for people of all ages and no previous knowledge of dancing is necessary. It gives the dancer plenty of exercise and the opportunity to meet new friends, both at the weekly classes and the various social events throughout the year.

The lady is always to the right of the man in the couple.

Old Time Square Dancing

Keeping Ulster-Scots Traditional Dances Alive

by Philip Robinson and Will McAvoy

ORIGINALLY PUBLISHED IN ULLANS NUMMER 3, SPRING 1995

T he survival of the Ulster-Scots traditional square dance is largely due to the work of one woman and her dancing class at Killinchy, County Down. Mrs Jeannie Peak was brought up in Ardmillan, near Killinchy. Her mother and father were very keen dancers, and she learned polkas, two-steps, the Lancers, Quadrilles and Caledonians from her parents as a young girl. The old-time square dances (Lancers, Quadrilles and Caledonians) were well known throughout the countryside one or two generations ago. People danced and learned to dance in the farmhouse kitchens. Mrs Peak remembers all these square dances being danced in Ardmillan Orange Hall and elsewhere. A small building beside the present Orange Hall, which had been the old Hall, was so small that when the fiddlers called the Lancers, there was room for only one 'set' of four couples at a time. When it had finished, the next set would get up and take its turn. The dances at Ardmillan Orange Hall have included these country square dances right until today without a break, and the Caledonians have always been the favourite. Had Mrs Peak not almost single-handedly taken on the job of teaching the dances to the present generation just as she had learnt them, almost certainly this tradition would have died out.

For the uninitiated, the 'square' dance consists of eightsome 'sets' of four couples, each with the dancers facing the centre of a small square. The lady is always to the right of the man in the couple forming each side of the square. The term 'set dancing' is not used in the Ulster-Scots tradition, but the dances are usually referred to by their individual names – the Caledonians, Lancers, Quadrilles, and so on. A 'set' is the formation of four couples in any of these dances, and so you can have 3, 4, or more sets on the floor. 'Old-time square dances' seems to be the name these dances are called nowadays, although 60 years ago they would not have been thought of as 'old-time'. Mrs Peak uses this name partly because 'square-dance' by itself is now usually taken to mean the American square dance (with a 'caller'), the type we are all familiar with. Of course, both the American and our own square dances are descended from exactly the same tradition. The Quadrille is the oldest and probably the original square dance. Sometimes it was called the 'Quad-reel' in County Down, perhaps because some thought of it as a 'square' version of the older Scotch reels. In the early 1700s our ancestors played a card-game called quadrilles, which had four couples playing each other seated on each side of a square table. The Quadrille as a name for the country dance appears in Ulster for the first time only during the early 1800s. Most people assume that the Caledonians, Lancers, and the American square dances developed from the Quadrille (which after all means a 'square' in French). It looks likely that the American variety sprang from among the Ulster-Scots settlers in the southern states (the 'Scotch-Irish' as they are known there). The term 'old-time square dance' is preferred as a name also to distinguish it from the Irish 'set dance' tradition. Although there are some similarities between the Irish set dances and the old-time square dances, the practitioners of the latter are adamant that these are not the same thing.

Each square dance consists of a number of 'figures' (usually five or six). These figures are separate dances within the dance, each with its own tune, a pause between, and its own sequence of steps. At the beginning of each 'figure' the couples 'honour their partners' during the first eight bars of music by bowing to each other, then turning and bowing again to the person of the opposite sex on their other side. During one of the movements when the dancers pass through each other (the 'chain'), it is important that the men and women smile at each other, ie 'Scottish Country Dancing style'.

How did Mrs Peak's classes start? Over 20 years ago the minister of Killinchy Presbyterian Church asked Mrs Peak if the Women's Group would arrange some music for a social night in the Church Hall. The two musicians she got were Jim Martin on the accordion and Willie M'Keag (from Carrowdore) on the tin whistle. During the night Mrs Peak and others got up to dance with the music, after which the minister's wife said she enjoyed it immensely, and she asked if Mrs Peak would start a class. So the usual Presbyterian objections to dancing in the church hall were overcome. The first dancing classes at Killinchy were held over the winter, from September on, and since then it has continued as a 'dance' but with old-time square dances always being called. The Killinchy winter dances moved to Ardmillan Orange Hall nine years ago.

About 17 years ago dances were started by Mrs Peak also in Raffery Orange Hall over the summer months, lasting from April until September, when the Killinchy classes started again. The Raffery dances still continue during the summer months, with almost all of the 'square' dancers there that can do the Caledonians and Quadrilles having been taught by Mrs Peak.

At the first Raffery old-time square dances the music was supplied by Jackie Donnan (fiddle) and a guitarist from Killyleagh. Shortly thereafter a band consisting of Owen Moore (accordion), Jim Muirhead (banjo and guitar), James Savage (fiddle), Caroline Berrow (fiddle), Addie McVea (fiddle) and Walter Frazer (drums) took over for the next four or five years. From then up to the present Samuel Miskelly with his piano-accordion has been playing at Raffery, and the dances now keep going all year round (Wednesdays, every fortnight). In the beginning only two or three couples knew the old square dances, apart from the 50 or 60 that came from Killinchy with Mrs Peak for the summer months.

The old-time dances that are favourites include 'sequence' dances such as the Pride of Erin, two-steps, waltzes and polkas such as the Heel and Toe Polka, the Plain Polka and the Polka Mazurka. Of course, it is the square dances such as the Quadrilles, Caledonians and Lancers that are the most popular, and it is these which would have died out had Mrs Peak's classes not kept them alive. Other square dances performed less regularly include the Waltz Cotillion and the D'Albert.

For a short time, Mrs Peak's class was held at Kilmood, on a Tuesday night. This followed the Kilmood Fiddlers Night on Monday nights, which still continues, but years back Kilmood had its own class for the Quadrilles organised by some of the local Church of Ireland parishioners. Other new classes were started under Mrs Peak, from Greyabbey in County Down to Ballyclare in County Antrim.

Can these 'old-time' square dances be regarded as 'traditional' Ulster-Scots country dances? There isn't a clear-cut answer to that question. Certainly all the 'square' dances, including some of the modern 'Irish set' dances and the American square dances, seem to have a single origin in the Quadrille, a dance supposedly introduced from France to the British Isles about 1816. The Lancers and the Caledonians presumably developed very soon afterwards as variations of the Quadrilles, and these three dances were popular throughout the British Isles and America at the end of the nineteenth century. Of course, that did not mean that the Quadrilles or the Lancers were danced in the same way in County Down as they were in Ayrshire, Shropshire or County Cork. Each district must have developed its own local styles, for they are not exactly the same in each area today.

How far back can we trace these square dances in the Ulster-Scots areas of Antrim and Down? For the best records we must go back to over 150 years ago, when map-makers from the Ordnance Survey prepared a whole series of written descriptions of parishes throughout Ireland, descriptions which included the 'habits, customs and amusements' of local inhabitants. Ulster was covered by Ordnance Survey Memoirs during the 1830s, and these Memoirs spell out very clearly which parishes were peopled with Ulster-Scots, most of them being in counties Antrim and Down. (The original manuscript memoirs have been mostly transcribed and republished on a parish-by-parish basis, eg Angélique Day and Patrick McWilliams (eds.)

Ordnance Survey Memoirs of Ireland Vol. 17: Parishes of County Down IV – East Down and Lecale [Belfast and Dublin: Institute of Irish Studies, QUB, and The Royal Irish Academy, 1992].) The Surveyors preparing the Memoirs were English, Anglo-Irish, or Irish and had a surprising hostility towards the Ulster-Scots. For example, in the Parish of Carnmoney to the north of Belfast we find the following commentary:

> There is scarcely a tradition in the parish. This is not much to
> be wondered, when it is remembered that but 2 centuries have
> elapsed since their ancestors first settled in the country. ...
> There is not any ancient music in the parish. Their airs and
> ballads are merely those commonly known in the country, and
> are strictly Scottish. ... Their accent is peculiarly, and among the
> old people disagreeably, strong and broad. Their idioms and
> saws are strictly Scottish. Four-fifths of the population of this
> parish are Presbyterians. ... The Covenanters worship at the
> meeting house in the hamlet of Carnmoney. ... They are still by
> some styled the 'Cameronians' or 'mountainy people' and are
> believed to retain usages of the ancient original Scottish church.

As far as dancing was concerned, the Memoir for Carnmoney does make mention of Quadrilles:

> Dancing is their favourite amusement. Scarce a month passes
> without there being a dance in some of the farmers' houses,
> either in this parish or in those immediately adjoining it.
> Reels, country dances and sometimes quadrilles are the usual
> figures. The violin is the usual instrument, but the Highland
> pipes are also sometimes introduced. They dance pretty well
> and rather lightly. The refreshment consists of punch and
> biscuits. The dances got up among the factory people are
> not by any means conducted with the same propriety
> as those at the farmers' houses.

The Parish of Carnmoney in the 1830s ran to the outskirts of north Belfast and included Whitehouse, so here alone is mention made of dances 'got up among the factory people'. Throughout Counties Antrim and Down, wherever the population was described as 'Scotch', dancing is given as the most popular, and sometimes the only, amusement.

From the Parish of Templecorran (east Antrim) we read:

> Formerly Dances in this and the surrounding Parishes, but particularly in Islandmagee are of frequent occurrence and were very numerously attended.... Their accent idioms and phraseology are strictly and disagreeably Scottish partaking only of the broad and coarse accent and dialect of the Southern Counties of Scotland... They have not any national music, their songs are merely the common ballads of the County and their airs like those of the Northern Counties are Scottish.

From the Parish of Islandmagee (east Antrim):

> They have not any particular recreation, but all their sports are of a Scottish character. Dancing seems to be the favourite. 'Punch dances' at public houses and dances given in the farmers barns, once a frequent occurrence, are now few and far between. They are fond of listening to music, the violin is their favourite instrument. The inhabitants, being all of a Scotch descent ... retain the manners and habits of their ancestors. ... The people are very hospitable, but very blunt in their manners and obstinate in their opinions.

From the Parish of Grange of Ballywalter (east Antrim):

> Attending a dance, idling a day or two at Christmas and Easter and going to 2 or 3 of the summer fairs are now their own recreations. All the names are purely Scottish. The family of Shaw is said to be the most ancient in the grange. Almost the entire population are Presbyterians, there being scarcely a member of the Churches of England or Rome. There is no party spirit, but there is a strong prejudice against Protestantism [ie the established, episcopal Church of Ireland] and Popery.

The Parish of Mallusk, although also in east Antrim, was in a similar position to Carnmoney, as it also flanked the north of Belfast. Only in Carnmoney and Mallusk is there mention of Quadrilles, so if they were introduced to the British Isles only 10-15 years previously, perhaps they were only starting to spread into the Ulster-Scots countryside during the 1830s.

From the Parish of Mallusk (east Antrim):

> Dancing is a very favourite amusement. ... There are still several annual dances in this and the neighbouring districts. Those in the library at the hamlet of Roughfort in the parish of Templepatrick are among the most fashionable and are nicely got up. Among the better description of farmers the assistance and services of a dancing master are indispensable, while among the lower class a few steps accidentally picked up are quite sufficient, with their naturally good taste and ears, to ensure their excelling in this lively accomplishment.
>
> Among the farmers, quadrilles, country dances and reels, and with the lower class the 2 latter figures are at present in vogue. Their dances, whether subscription or private, are in general nicely got up and are conducted with decorum and propriety. The parties come in full dress, and in their hours of breaking up imitate the example of their superiors. ...
>
> There is much taste for music, but they have not any other than the common airs of the country. The violin is the favourite instrument with the men and several perform on it. ... Their dialect, accent, idioms and customs are strictly Scottish, and among the old people are many homely and pithy old saws and proverbs. ... [There is] little or no party spirit. They are almost equally prejudiced against property and tithes. They are independent almost to bigotry towards any other persuasion [than Presbyterian]. They are rather rough and blunt.

The mention of 'dancing masters' in Mallusk is repeated for the Parish of Kilwaughter (east Antrim):

> Dancing is the only amusement. There are occasional dances in the farmhouses of the parish, and at present a dancing school has just commenced. It consists of about 6 pupils, each pay 5s per quarter, chiefly females attend.

Throughout the rest of County Antrim, less detail is given about what dances were performed, but wherever dancing is highlighted as the principal amusement, the inhabitants are always described as being 'Scottish' and with 'Scotch customs and music'.

From the Parish of Carncastle and Killyglen (east Antrim):

> Cards, dancing and cock-fighting are the principal amusements. … [The people are] too thoroughly Scotch to allow any patron's [Saints] days. The inhabitants still retain the Scottish habits and accent.

From the Parish of Drumtullagh (north Antrim):

> … peopled by the descendants of the Scottish and English emigrants. The Scotch language is spoken in great purity. … Dancing and a little cock-fighting are their principal amusements.

From the Parish of Billy (north Antrim):

> … fond of dancing.

From the Parish of Derrykeighan (north Antrim):

> … principal amusements are dancing and a little cock-fighting.

From the Parish of Ballyrashane (north Londonderry):

Dances occasionally take place.

From the Parish of Aghanloo (north Londonderry):

The local customs most prevalent are the same as what are
prevalent among all Scottish inhabitants of the country...
dancing is a favourite amusement... they seem to be very fond
of fiddle playing. Singing schools are held in rotation among
the Presbyterian farmers' houses and after music, both sacred
and profane, a dance generally concludes.

From the Parish of Dundermot (Antrim):

... dancing is the only amusement ... inhabitants all descendants
of the Scotch Presbyterians.

From the Parish of Racavan (Antrim):

... dancing and singing parties ... the great mass of the
population are Presbyterian.

From the Parish of Grange of Shilvoden (Antrim):

... inhabitants display disagreeable Scottish manners ... dancing
now nearly given up.

From the Parish of Ahoghill (Antrim):

Cock-fighting, card-playing and dances, which formerly were
numerously attended, are now, except the latter, and it very
seldom, never known among that body ... owing to the
exertions of their clergy ... inhabitants much resemble the
Scots in their habits, customs and dialect. They are rather
dogged, obstinate and blunt.

From the Parish of Armoy (north Antrim):

> They seem to be almost exclusively of Scottish extraction ...
> The inhabitants towards the more mountainous parts are very
> uncouth and ignorant. ... Their principal amusement is dancing.

From the Parish of Ballintoy (north Antrim):

> They are all the descendants of the Scottish settlers of the 16th
> century, as may be inferred from their very broad Scotch dialect
> and accent. ... Except dancing, they cannot be said to have any
> particular amusement.

From the Parish of Ramoan (north Antrim):

> Dancing forms the principal amusement of the lower class and
> in this they indulge frequently, particularly at the fairs and large
> markets in Ballycastle, at which time there is generally a room
> in each public house set apart for that purpose.

From the Parish of Connor (Antrim):

> Dancing is their only amusement. Dancing and singing parties
> are the principal resort in the evenings.

Accounts of other Ulster-Scots parishes in Antrim, including Finvoy, Killygen, Kirkinriola, Skerry and Drummaul, all contain a single brief reference to 'a little dancing', 'dancing their only amusement' and so on. When the Ordnance Surveyors wrote the Memoirs for County Down, they made mention of the same sort of things as in County Antrim in the parishes where the inhabitants were 'Scotch'. Unfortunately, they did not seem to make notes about what sort of recreations were enjoyed. One exception was the Parish of Greyabbey:

> The country people appear fond of dancing, some of whom are
> proficient in a description of reel. An annual ball takes place in
> the village about the month of July. It appears to be exclusively
> Masonic. ... The inhabitants are almost exclusively Presbyterian.

These Ordnance Survey Memoirs establish beyond any doubt that during the 1830s the same areas that are 'Ulster-Scots' today were even more strikingly 'Scotch' in those days. Dancing was easily the most popular Ulster-Scots tradition, the music usually being provided by a fiddler, but sometimes by the 'Highland pipes'. Everything about these people seemed strangely and stubbornly 'Scotch' to the Surveyors, and this applied no less to their music and dancing. References to Reels, 'Country Dances' and 'sometimes Quadrilles' give us only a glimpse of the nature of the dances themselves. The Lancers and the Caledonians are not mentioned, but that is what might be expected if these square dances developed later from the Quadrilles. We cannot tell what the old 'country dances' were, but they may well have provided the originals for the oldest of the dances now preserved by the Royal Scottish Country Dance Society.

The Quadrilles and other old-time dances may have started off as fashionable 'new' dances. However, they must have blended in very quickly with the older country dances. From the beginning they were danced to Scotch tunes, picking up the local steps, variation and styles. They were danced in farmhouses as well as in larger buildings.

It is difficult to turn the clock back much before the 1830s to see what dances were traditional to the Ulster-Scots before the 'square' dances became popular. Samuel Thomson, the bard of Carngranny (near Carnmoney), published his first book of Ulster-Scots poems in 1793. There are casual references to dances throughout, such as in his 'Elegy to my Auld Shoen':

> Nae mair my social hours ye'll dree;
> Nae mair ye'll scour the daisied lee;
> Nae mair to dance ye'll carry me,
> Nor ever mair
> Those happiest of my minutes see
> Beside my fair.

One of his poems, however, was called 'The Country Dance' and was 16 verses long. Only one brief passage gives any clue to the dances:

> At countra' dances, jigs and reels
> Alternatively they ranted,

although in a different verse he says

Now o'er the floor in wanton pairs,
They foot it to the fiddle;
The maidens muster a' their airs,
The young men skip an' striddle.

The rest of the poem, like most of the other Ulster-Scots poetry that mentions country dancing, concentrates almost exclusively on the fun, games and exploits that surrounded the occasions. Naturally it never occurred to them that 200 years later we might be interested to know what the actual dances were!

Many of the 'old-time' dances that are still popular today were 'new' dances in the 1850s and 1860s – dances such as the polkas (of which many 'country' versions now exist), the many 'old-time' dances based on the waltz, and of course the old-time square dances such as the Lancers, Caledonians, the D'Albert and later still the Waltz Cotillion. About 1870, a generation after the Ordnance Survey Memoirs were written, the Lancers, Quadrilles and Caledonians were well established. One of the best-known Ulster-Scots poets from County Down during that era, Robert Huddleston of Moneyreagh, wrote no fewer than four lengthy poems about dancing: 'The Dance at Paddy's Toun', 'The Dancing', 'The Dancing School', and 'The Dancing Night'. Despite the fact that he penned page after page of broad Ulster-Scots poetry about dancing – over 1000 lines in these four poems alone – Huddleston didn't have much to say about the actual types of dances performed. In his earliest poem, 'The Dancing Night', written about 1848, only four of the 800 lines tell us anything at all:

And figures money they did dance
Baith English Iris Scotch an French
...
Now dancin went on wae merry fun
And fiddles did roar like a gun.

In 'The Dance at Paddy's Toun', one line went 'set on set thus squared the floor'. Elsewhere we read:

Cuts and capers odd frae France
Joy did a' the folk entrance
          Danced and spreed at Paddy's Dance
...

> Up they got a jig to dance
> Span-new braw frae Bawdy's Toun:
> Up they got - the Band went strang,
> At the *'Pushing Step'* they're thrang.

One completely different poem of Huddleston's, 'Ye nobles a o Parliament', has a passing mention of the 'aul quadrill':

> Let Wellinton blaw lood an shrill
> Till he dis scarr baith knowt an Bill
> By dancin up they aul *quadrill*
> Or who the scampt aff Bunkers hill.

Most of the limited amount of information Huddleston gives us comes from his poem 'The Dancing':

> The fiddler now is just arrived
>
> ...
>
> A meikle carle grim and bauld
> To dance and sing the *Heelin Fling*
> As a' they're dancing roun' him
>
> ...
>
> And while pantin' and gauntin'
> For breath some take the door
> E'en sprucely and crucely
> Some others *square the floor*
>
> ...
>
> And on the danced till a' they peght
> And scoured the floor baith right and left
> *Set after set*, like weaver's weft
> And aye the crossed and cleekit
> And *reels* and *gigs* and *figures* wro'ght
> And *hornpipes* too wi' merry a'ght
> Till a' are tired 'fore and aft'
> And they all reeked and sweatit
>
> ...
>
> Now on the floor behold! the dance
> Whas up a *hornpipe* for to dance

> A *hornpipe* by a funny wench
> > As bad as bawdy lookin'
> Sae figity amid her fun
> Her steps they aye to striddles run
>
> ...
>
> And aye she bobbed wi' every step
> > As at it she would fain be
> While played the fiddler till he swet
> > And aired up Cockabendy.

Huddleston described in great detail just about everything else that happened at a dance – except the dancing – including the types of people there, the musicians, the courting, the ructions, the food and drink, the arguments and the party games. Just as is suggested in the Ordnance Survey Memoirs, there seems to have been little difference between a dancing and a singing class. In 'The Dancing', Huddleston describes some of the 'party games' (most of which were courtship or kissing games):

> Here some ride the *wooden* mare
> > And some are at *Blinharnet*
> And *sho'el the brogue* e'en try some mair
> > Wha ither sports for care not
> And while the fiddler's in the room
> > Wi' favourites yet a bousin
> See in the kitchen here's a gang
> > That muckle time's no loosin'.

In a poem called 'The Country Singing', John Dickey of Donegore (County Antrim) wrote in 1818 of one diversion, the 'frisky dance', and gave a note to explain it:

> The 'frisky dance' is now put round
> A rude-like scene indeed
>
> *NOTE: Six young women are set upon a form; then eight
> young men rise, seven of whom take hands in a round ring,
> whilst one sings in the middle as they dance round – 'The Friar
> he danced the frisky dance', etc. Thus, round they caper and
> chorus, till he in the middle sings out a watchword, at which

the seven youths fly like as many lions upon the fair creatures, each struggling for a kiss, because he that gets none is cobbed, that is, he is beat upon the soles of his feet with a piece of broad board, or a good tight shillelagh, which is to him a truely mortifying scene – such is the Frisky Dance.

B A Botkin's classic *Treasury of American Folklore*, published in 1944, has an entire section on 'Singing and Play-Party Games', which begins:

> In the field of the game and dance, two distinctive American developments from British sources are the square dance, quadrille, or cotillion (as distinguished from the English contra-dance or longways dance, which still persists in New England) and the play party. In the United States the term 'square dance' has come to stand for old-time sequence dancing generally, whether of the square, longways, or circle formation. Although the guitar and the banjo are used to accompany the fiddle at dances, as well as to accompany the folk singer, the fiddle is the American folk musical instrument par excellence. Because of religious prejudice against dancing and especially the fiddle, as the instrument of the devil, the young people of rural America developed the play party as an alternative form of amusement, which substituted singing for instrumental accompaniment. A cross between dancing and the traditional singing games of children, the play party retains the best features of both. To the courtship and other dramatic devices of the game, such as choosing and stealing partners, the play party adds certain square dance movements and figures, in which, however, partners are swung by the hands instead of by the waist.
>
> (Botkin, page 803)

It is clear to anyone familiar with the Ulster-Scots traditions of the nineteenth century that square dancing, singing and 'play parties' were all part of the scene in Antrim and Down 150 years ago. Today, of course, the old-time square dancers are respectable couples, and the 'play party' courtship games are reserved for children's and young people's gatherings – including, surprisingly enough, annual Sunday-School parties! One of the American games called 'Hog Drovers' is described by Botkin as 'originally an Irish game played at wakes'. He gives the song that is sung, and describes the game which (like the 'frisky dance' above) invokes a couple sitting on chairs in the middle of a room, other couples walking hand in hand round them, and a change of partners at the end of each verse. The last couple paired form a bridge by joining hands and the other couples pass through. Any imprisoned couples under the bridge must kiss. (Both authors of this article remember similar games at Sunday-School parties.) The Ulster-American connections with the traditional square dance, therefore, seem to be much deeper than just the dances themselves.

Let's come back to the square dance. John Stevenson, writing in *Pat McCarty, Farmer of Antrim: His Rhymes with a Setting* (1905), gives a description of the dancing after a 'quilting' party:

> Aweel – wi' grace on lassie's side and vigour on the men's,
> They danc'd in ev'ry step and time and custom o' the airt;
> And tho' they danc'd besides in ways nae dancin'-master kens
> The airm aroon' yer lassie's waist's the maist important pairt.

Another of his poems, 'The Dance at Widow Clarke's', makes mention of the 'waltz' (as if it was a new dance), the polka and the 'auld quadreel'.

> There's gaun to be some dancin' at Weeda Clarke's the day
>   I'm practeesin' the waltz
>   An' tho' wi' mony faults,
> I'm able noo to dae it in a sort o' kind o' way.
>   'It's no' a common dance;
>   It cam', they say, frae France
> Or Jarmany it may be - some far ootlandish way,
>   We'll no' brak up till three,
>   In fack it's gaun to be
> The kind o' enterteenment that the top o' gintry hae.
>   ...
>
>   'I ken the auld *quadreel*,
>   And polka middlin' weel,
> But whirlin' till yer dizzy is a deil's inventit way;
>   We spin roon' like a tap,
>   Until we're fit to drap,
> Then hap the way I'll show ye - as the titled gintry dae'.

Numerous other Ulster-Scots writers make mention of dancing in the country farmhouses, but they give very little information about the dances, preferring to concentrate on the social occasion as a whole. Quite simply, there is not enough information in the historical record for us to reconstruct now what way the 'country dances' and square dances such as the 'quadrilles' were actually danced over a century ago. The only way of catching a glimpse of these 'old-time' traditions of dancing is by witnessing the real thing in action.

But what is the real thing? In 1950 Victor Sylvester first published his book *Old Time Dancing*, which has become a classic. It includes the instructions for the whole range of square dances: the Lancers, the Quadrille, the Waltz Cotillion, and the Caledonians. But there is very little similarity between Victor Sylvester's version of these dances and how they are danced by Mrs Jeannie Peak's dancing class at Killinchy. The music and the steps are in completely different modes. Two generations ago, literally tens of thousands of people could have gone through the Ulster-Scots traditional square dance steps. Nowadays, but for a handful of people such as Mrs Peak who have kept these traditions alive, we would have no possibility of knowing anything at all about our very own dancing tradition.

This article has been written to point out the importance of the connections between the Ulster-Scots of America and Ireland, and as an acknowledgement of Mrs Peak's role in passing on knowledge of the square dances for another generation.

Lang-Bowls wes play't wi an iron ba.

The Bowls

by Philip Robinson
ORIGINALLY PUBLISHED IN ULLANS NUMMER 2, SPRING 1994

Whilk sports o wor ain wud we hae here in Ulster? Wud there be onie sairt o a traditional sport for the Ulster-Scotch? Ye cud say Shinty, seein it wes a bit like the Hurlin an monies an Ulster poet used tae mak mention o it. Mebbe yinst it micht a bin, bot wha's iver heerd o onie Shinty matches gettin playit noo-a-days? Fitba, ay, an mebbe motor-bike racin tae, hes aye pu'd mair fowk thegither nor onie ither sport ye cud mention. Thae wudnae be ca't 'traditional sports' bot, an the' hinnae much o a Scotch connection forbye. Bowls mair is the thing. Divil a Meetin-Hoose or toon in the hail kintra 'at hisnae gat a Bowlin Club, an a wheen o years back did Jim Baker no bear the gree o a World Title? The Bowlin gat a quare heft whan Jim brung thon title hame tae Coontie Antrim. Richt roon the wurl theday, the Bowls is organised wi rules set doon bi a boy fae Glesca, an Scotlan haes aye bin big wi Bowlin Clubs. O coorse, the Bowls gat a guid playin bi Sir Francis Drake in the days o Elizabeth I. In them days Carrickfergus hed its ain Bowlin Green tae, fur whan the wa's o Carrick toon wes biggit in 1618, the new wa cut the oul Bowlin Green in twa fornenst the North Gate.

Efter 1605, whan hordes o Scotchies come owre tae north Down fae Scotlan – alang wi the Big Plantin o Ulster – Bangor, Newton, an Comber wes near aa Scotch, an yin or twa o thae toons wes pit doon on wee maps made in 1625. Baith Bangor an Comber hed a 'Ball Greene' mairk't on thair plons in 1625. Sae, fur near fower hunner year the Bowls haes bin play't bi the Ulster-Scotch. Bot whit o the Long-Bowls or Bullets 'at gets play't alang the kintra loanens in the Coontie Armagh yit? Weel, there's a brave wheen o sic places in Antrim and Down 'at gets ca't the 'Lang-Shot', an thae airts used tae be gaitherin places fur Lang-Bowls. Map makers o the 1830s daein thair day's darg in South Antrim wud gie reports o Lang-Bowls, an way bak afore that, 'lang bullets' wes the favourite sport o the Rev Philip Skelton. He wes born in 1707 at Derriaghy, near Lisburn, an as a wee lad he cudnae be bate at the bullets bi oniebody in the Parish. Yinst he tuk a holiday tae the Mournes, an gat bate there bi a wee runt o a craytur.

The *Dictionary of the Older Scottish Tongue* makes mention o 'lang bowlis' in Scotlan bak in the fowerteen hunners. Seein Lang-Bowls wes play't wi an iron ba, it was aye gey an dangerous. Skelton in 1728 wes playin' long-bullets whan a three pun ba come fleein aff a stane an gied him a sair dunt on the heed. Ither folks ses thon dinge in his heid wes the cause o aa the daft things the wee meenister gat up tae efter.

The Bard o Moneyreagh, Bab Huddlestone, niver made much o a mention o Bowls in onie o his poems, bot in yin o his letters tae a freen in America, he toul him 'at he hed gat a hit on the shank fae a lang-bowl twal year afore an wes near a cripple syne. That was aboot the year 18 an 70, an he ax't his freen did he no min' the guid oul days the' used t'hae at the bullets whan the' was wee fellas.

The baith sairts o Bowls haes aye been the sport o the Ulster-Scotch bards. Ma ain favourite is James Orr, the Bard o Ballycarry, wha pit doon aboot the year 1800 a poetic epistle tae anither great bard, Samuel Thomson o Carngranny. Orr ends up wi thir lines:

> I'll hae to quat my humble strains
> The moon-beams gild my frost-wrought anes
>   An' I've a bit to gang:
> I hope your muirlan muse ye'll woo
> To tell me how ye wrastle thro',
>   Some time when ye're no thrang
> Atween an' May, gif bowls row right
>   I'll meet ye in Roughfort
> An' aince again devote a night
>   To Frien'liness an' sport.

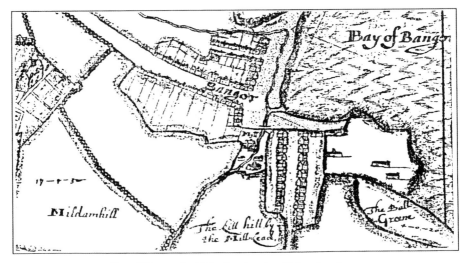

Map of Bangor in 1625, showing the old Bowling Green

Little girls were introduced to embroidery from an early age, perhaps as young as five or six.

Ayrshire Needlework in the Ards

by Linda M Ballard
ORIGINALLY PUBLISHED IN ULLANS NUMMER 6, SPRING 1998

As the name implies, Ayrshire needlework originated in Scotland. It is credited to a Mrs Jamieson, wife of a merchant, whose close study and unpicking of a piece of French embroidery is said to have led to her establishing a new craft skill and trade in her home area in the early nineteenth century. Certainly large quantities of beautiful white embroidery of this type were produced in Scotland in the first half of the nineteenth century, and Mrs Jamieson is listed as one of the ladies taking orders in or before 1830. By that date, Ayrshire work (for which needleworkers could be trained in three months) was being 'put out' to women in the Ards Peninsula of County Down.

The primary reasons for its prevalence in the Ards Peninsula were the short sea crossing and close commercial and social contacts between the east coast of Ireland and the west of Scotland, particularly between Portpatrick and Donaghadee. It seems there was a ready capacity among local women to produce this lovely form of embroidery, which was in great demand as a fashionable type of decoration for garments and accessories for women and for children. Perhaps the most common sort of garment in which Ayrshire work survives is the christening or *dookin* gown, often passed through generations of a family. White garments were considered since ancient times to be essential for this ceremony, but the Ayrshire decorated dresses which continue in wear may not originally have had solely ritual uses, but may have been kept for conspicuous best wear in an era when these were fashionable.

For needlework enthusiasts, or perhaps for the owner of an heirloom christening dress, it may be useful to describe the characteristics of Ayrshire work. It is technically a very demanding form of embroidery. It is done with white thread, generally on high quality muslin lawn of exceptional fineness: in other words, on a cotton rather than a linen base. It is worth remembering that it is typical of the early part of the nineteenth century, when cotton production flourished and when this was widely woven even locally. Designs are beautiful and elegant, and while themes are often drawn from nature, the patterns are generally classical and quite stylised in appearance. The work is small in scale and often densely embroidered over the ground. Much of the design is worked in satin stitch, but other stitches are also employed, as are beautiful lace work fillings, which may feature either pulled thread work or filled stiletto piercings. Sometimes the decorative filling stitches are replaced with insertions of darned net. Button hole stitch is essential, as edges and scallops are finished with tiny work of this sort.

Ayrshire work was established in the Donaghadee area by 1830, when the firm of Cochrane was distributing fabric for embroidery to local women. Women worked in their own homes, fitting in their needlework along with their many other chores and duties, and embroidery often made a very substantial contribution to family income. Indeed, families headed by widows may have found themselves dependent on the mothers' abilities as fine needlewomen. Little girls were introduced to embroidery from an early age, perhaps as young as five or six. Embroideresses received all work stamped out on flat sheets of fabric, so that an entire christening gown would be marked out for completion. The hem even of the back of the very full and ultimately finely gathered skirt, usually scalloped and often with a design of tiny satin stitch dots or of similar work, would have to be buttonholed, in addition to working the elaborate decoration for the front panels of bodice and skirt. Sleeves and front flounces (which are usually referred to as *robings*) would also be embroidered. The local agent or manufacturer would hand out the work – collars, baby caps, handkerchiefs or whatever was currently in demand – and would generally collect this a week later, delivering fresh work and issuing payment for finished work. Sometimes embroideresses received their payment not in cash but in kind, bartering their needlework for a week's groceries. There has been quite a lot of controversy about whether or not needlewomen worked outdoors when weather permitted, but it seems very likely that they took advantage of the sunshine when they could. In Scotland reference is made to the *Floo'erin Stanes* on which they sat outside their homes in order to do their embroidery. *Floo'erin* makes reference to the picturesque term *flowering*, by which embroidery is often known, a term which relates both to the floral subjects often featured in embroidery design and to the fact that fabric is embellished by the addition of embroidery.

By the early 1830s, Cochrane had established a business in Glasgow, in cooperation with another merchant called Brown, so the potential for Ayrshire embroidery in County Down and beyond must have been very considerable by this comparatively early date. Among the important developments for which Cochrane and Brown were responsible seems to have been the discovery of a method of using lithography to print embroidery designs onto fabric. This appears to have happened in or around 1837. Prior to this, wood blocks were generally used to stamp the design onto the material to be embroidered.

It is very clear that local women were highly skilled in the production of exquisite needlework in the decades before the Famine, and during the 1840s fine needlework continued to be produced. It is important to remember this fact, as there is a tendency to believe that high quality work could not have been made in Ireland at that date, a mistake which sometimes leads to local work being attributed to European, particularly French, sources. The fact that French needlework may have been the source upon which Ayrshire work was originally based would help to account for this, but travellers in pre-Famine Ireland noted the skills of local embroideresses and commented that their work equalled and often excelled that produced in France at the time. Embroidery was a highly specialised craft, so that a piece might be passed from needlewoman to needlewoman in order that each could work her own particular skill as required by the design. As many as seven people might contribute to the work on a high-quality handkerchief.

As with most fashions, the taste for Ayrshire work declined with the passage of time, and in the later nineteenth century other types of lace and embroidery became more popular. One reason for this was the invention in Switzerland of a machine which could copy the style of Ayrshire work quite closely, but much faster than the delicate and intricate handwork could be produced. Local women diversified, but their work often continued to be described as *floo'erin* or *flowering*, a skill for which the Ards Peninsula and other regions long retained a high reputation. It is clear that the skills specifically associated with Ayrshire work, especially in the glorious lace fillings, were not lost to the women of the Ards. Early in the twentieth century, a Belfast linen firm produced a magnificent cambric linen cloth decorated with an embroidered border of peacocks, peacocks in their pride being stitched into each corner. Peacocks became popular as a design motif for embroidery in the 1890s, and the cloth referred to, which is now in the collection of the National Museums and Galleries of Northern Ireland situated at Cultra, uses them in a wonderful and fashionable *art nouveau* pattern. The tails of the peacocks are worked using the filled stiletto piercings which feature so magnificently in Ayrshire work, and the cloth was passed from embroideress to embroideress, just as earlier pieces were. It is known that the embroidery was done by women from the Ards area, and one of them, a fisherman's wife, Martha Cooper, is personally remembered as having done some of the fine work. Appropriately, the French connection was maintained, as the cloth was exhibited and took a prize in Paris.

OLD

Scottish Psalm Tunes

*A Supplement to Existing Psalmodies, with Table
of Adaptations for the most commonly used
Psalms and Paraphrases*

REVISED AND ENLARGED EDITION
SOL-FA NOTATION

BAYLEY & FERGUSON
LONDON: 2 GREAT MARLBOROUGH STREET, W.
GLASGOW: 54 QUEEN STREET

Practice Verses for Psalm Tunes

by William Robb
ORIGINALLY PUBLISHED IN ULLANS NUMMER 3, SPRING 1995

> There wuz an old seceeder cat
> And it wus unco grey
> It brung a moose intil the hoose
> Upon the Sabbath Day
>
> They tuk it tae the Session
> Wha it rebuikit sair
> An made it promise faithfully
> Tae dae the same nae mair
>
> An noo a' Sabbath Day it sits
> Like some oul clockin hen
> An cannae unnerstaun ava
> The ways o mice and men

This three-verse poem is an example of a type of verse which was used to enable choirs of Presbyterian churches in Scotland and Ireland during the eighteenth and nineteenth centuries to practise the tunes of metrical psalms. The first Psalter used in Irish Presbyterianism was the Scottish Psalter of 1564. A revised version of this published in 1650 was used up to 1880, when it was replaced in Ireland by the Irish Psalter, which is still current although its use has now declined considerably because of the inclusion of a large number of metrical psalms in the current (Third) Edition of the Church Hymnary.

The First Edition of the Church Hymnary appeared in 1899. Up to that date psalms were the only musical component of public worship in Presbyterian churches, on the grounds that it was proper to sing only words taken from the Scripture. A 'half-way house' between psalms and hymns had appeared in the nineteenth century when a book of 'paraphrases', ie passages of Scripture other than the psalms paraphrased into verse form, was published. It should be noted that for many years the psalms were sung unaccompanied by an organ, again on the grounds that there was no Scriptural authority for the use of instruments. The controversy over the use of organs is, however, another story.

The strict view that only psalms should be used in worship was further emphasised by the view that the actual words of the psalms should be used only in Sabbath services and should not be used in choir practices for the purpose of learning the tunes. It is, of course, normal for choirs to learn new tunes by singing them to 'la' until they know the tune well enough to fit it to the words. But the use of 'la' throughout an entire choir practice would be very monotonous, and so a number of 'practice verses' were composed in both Scotland and Ireland to enable choirs to learn new tunes. These verses varied from place to place: some were obviously of local origin, some were pure doggerel, and some showed a considerable degree of humour.

The greater number of metrical psalms were written in what was known as 'common metre' (the same as 'ballad metre' in general poetry), ie in four-line verses with the accents 4, 3, 4, 3. Some were written in 'long metre' ie 4, 4, 4, 4, while some were written in 'short metre', ie 3, 3, 4, 3. Some practice verses were regarded as belonging to particular tunes, but, as there were probably fewer practice verses than the number of psalms (150), some must have been used for more than one tune. Here are some examples. It will be noted that these verses are mostly in normal English, which is perhaps inevitable (despite the common use of dialect), as the Bible itself was in English.

Sung to the tune 'York'
The name of this tune is called York,
  The reason I don't know;
They might as well have called it Cork,
  Carmarthen or Raphoe.

Sung to the tune 'London'
Oh! London, thou art threatened sore
  By France to pull thee down,
But Providence is thy defence,
  Thou city of renown.

Sung to the tune 'Dublin'
In Ireland doth fair Dublin stand,
  The city chief therein;
And it is said by many more
  The city chief of sin.

A verse from north Down:

> There is a hill called Scrabo Hill
> Which hides my love from me:
> I'll bore a hole through Scrabo Hill
>   And then my love I'll see.

Some examples of humour:

> As I was coming here tonight
>   A wonder I did see;
> An ear(i)wig sat on a bush
>   And it threw stones at me.

> Young man, your head I do compare
>   Unto a lemon skin
> Which weather-beaten is without
>   And empty is within.

> A saucy girl who had straight eyes
>   Came here our singing to despise;
> She left her manners at the school
>   And came up here to play the fool.

Romance is not unknown among choir members:

> Within this room I do behold
>   A maid of beauty bright;
> And if I had ten thousand pounds
>   I'd share with her this night.

But it is not always reciprocated:

> The fair one here of whom you sing
>   She values not your coin,
> For if ten thousand more you'd bring
>   She would not with you join.

Based on church history:

> This is the tune the martyrs sang
>   When they were going to die,
> When they were to the scaffold brought
>   The truth to testify.
>
> Beneath the Alps Savoy doth stand
>   And Piedmont valley doth command;
> There the Waldenses felt the stroke
>   Of Papal power and Papal yoke.

The poem cited at the beginning of this article is an example in Scottish dialect. The first two verses are traditional. The third was written by the founder and conductor of the world famous Glasgow Orpheus Choir, Sir Hugh Roberton, who to the tune 'Desert' made it a favourite item in their repertoire under the title 'Mice and Men'.

The use of practice verses died out towards the end of the nineteenth century for a number of possible reasons. The introduction of a hymnary with a large number of hymns in many different metres to pre-set tunes rendered the use of practice verses obsolete. Then there is the difficulty that only by practising a tune to the actual words to which it is to be sung on Sunday can a proper fit between words and music be achieved. Finally, there is no reason why music rehearsed by a choir on a Thursday evening cannot be sung in as worshipful a frame of mind (even if less formal) as at a Sunday service.

Magee re-set the press and carried on printing.

Burns Corner:
The Early Belfast Printings

by Jim Heron
ORIGINALLY PUBLISHED IN ULLANS NUMMER 3, SPRING 1995

T he year 1786 was a highly significant one in the life of the 27-year-old Robert Burns, disillusioned with the long hours and heart-breaking toil that went with tenant farming. He seriously considered emigration to the West Indies, where he had been offered a job as a shipping clerk. Burns went as far as enquiring about a passage on the ship Nancy, which was due to sail towards the end of August from the port of Leith to Jamaica. In an attempt, however, to raise a few pounds, Burns sent a selection of his poems for publication to John Wilson, a Kilmarnock printer, who on 31 July 1786 put just over 600 copies up for sale at three shillings each.

Burns and Wilson were quite unprepared for the consequences of their creation, as the poetry began to take Scotland by storm, projecting Burns virtually overnight from common ploughman to literary genius. With thoughts of immigration now abandoned, Burns set off for Edinburgh on a borrowed pony. The journey took two days, and when he arrived, he found himself at the centre of attraction of a group of enlightened men of letters who had been making Edinburgh an internationally known intellectual centre. Indeed, at this time there were many who claimed Edinburgh as the cultural capital of Europe.

Over the next few weeks no smart party was complete unless the ploughman poet was in attendance. The poems found equal favour in all ranks of society, as the book was snapped up in farmhouses and cottages as well as country mansions. The first Edinburgh edition was published by William Creech on 21 April 1787, the printer being William Smelie, who also had been the editor and principal author of the first *Encyclopaedia Brittanica*. Whereas Burns had earned around £30 for the Kilmarnock edition, he now found his earnings for the Edinburgh edition exceeding £850.

From the third publisher of his works, however, Burns was to receive not a penny. The poetry of Burns hit the streets of Ulster during the latter half of 1786, when the *Belfast Newsletter* carried a number of pieces taken from the Kilmarnock edition. The poetry also became the main talking point among a number of small literary societies that had sprung up within the province. James Magee, a shrewd if somewhat unscrupulous Belfast printer, saw a way of making money out of all the euphoria, and on 24 September 1787 he published two hundred copies of the poetry taken straight from the Edinburgh edition. Inside ten days all copies were sold, so Magee re-set the press and carried on printing. These of course were all pirated copies (pirated in the respect that Burns was not to receive a penny by way of royalties).

Magee became quite a successful businessman in the town and in 1792 helped finance a Belfast newspaper, the *Northern Star*. He lived into his ninety-second year, and when he died he was buried in his native Craigavad. His shop was at No 11 Bridge Street, Belfast, just opposite the present Northern Ireland Electricity offices. He called his shop the Crown and Bible Printers, which probably reflected his religious and political persuasion. From his shop he sold musical instruments, patent medicines, state lottery tickets and of course the products of his printing press. In 1787 his Belfast edition of Burns poems was his best seller.

Incidentally, the first Belfast edition can be seen in Burns Cottage, at Alloway in Scotland. Other early editions of Burns in Ulster were:

J Magee (1787, 1790, 1793, 1800); Archer Ward (1805); L Rae (1814); Joseph Smith (1818); A McDonald (1816); and Simms & McIntyre (1822).

In 1992 Blackstaff Press in Belfast published two novels on the life and loves of Robert Burns.

In seiventaen an ninety-three Burns writ doon the wards uv twa sangs, frae Jean Glover.

Jean Glover and Letterkenny

by Conal Gillespie
ORIGINALLY PUBLISHED IN ULLANS NUMMER 6, SPRING 1998

It aye struck me as gey funny that the mair monie fowk is interested in the poems an sangs o' Rabbie Burns, onie a wee wheen o' oor Ulster Burnsmen, an weemin forebye, knaw aboot Jean Glover. In seiventaen an ninety-three Burns writ doon the wards uv twa sangs, 'Act Sederant of the Session' an 'O'er the Moor amang the Heather' frae Jean Glover, wha Burns cried 'a whore from Kilmarnock … stealing through the country with a slight of hand blackguard' (frae a note in Burns's ain copie o *The Scots Musical Museum*). In Burns's *Remarks on Scottish Songs*, Burns writ that Jean Glover 'was not only a whore but also a thief; and in one or other character has visited most of the correction houses in the west. She was born I believe in Kilmarnock – I took the song down from her singing …' (gien a mention i' the *Works of Robert Burns* ed. Allan Cunningham, Edinburgh 1870).

In nineteen an ninety-sax Billy Kay, wha writ S*cots – The Mither Tongue*, came ower till Belfawst tae spake. He made mention uv Jean Glover and reckoned that she crossed the sheugh tae Ulster. This wheen o wittens aboot Jeanie Glover set me delvin fur mair newis tae dae wi Burns's informant efter she come tae Ulster. Frae the buek *Ballads and Songs of Ayrshire* (nae date), i' the Dick Institute ben Kilmarnock I jaloused that Jeanie Glover dee'd i' the toon uv Letterkenny fernenst the Laggan in aist Donegal. Frae the buek I foun oot that Jeanie Glover wuz boarn i' the Toonheid uv Kilmarnock in seiventaen an fiftie echt. She wuz guid luckin an a gey guid singer. Jeanie wuz fand uv the roamin players wha betimes cam tae the toon an tuk up wi yin uv a company cried Richard, the 'slight of hand blackguard' wha Burns writ aboot. She striddlet aboot the wast uv Scotlan an sung at fairs fur a wheen o yeirs. Yin mon wha see'd her in Scotlan went on fur a sodger an wuz sent ayont tae Airlan tae the berrick i' Letterkenny. He see'd Jeanie liltin i' tha toon. Seein as how he knowed her, he put spake on Jeanie an foun her 'in good health, gay and sprightly as when in her native country'. This wuz the yeir echteen hunner an wan. This mon stayet i' Letterkenny fur twa montht. Afore he quat the toon Jeanie Glover 'was mouldering in silent dust'. She maun a deed sudden i' or aboot Letterkenny an been buriet i' yin uv the buryin gruns there aboot.

It's no small consait tae me that the Laggan, which wuz hame til a braw clatter uv oor Ulster Scotch rhymers, is connectit wi a wummin wha gied sangs til Burns.

Curling accompanied the settlers to Ireland during the reign of James I.

The Sport of Curling in Ulster

by Andrew Steven
ORIGINALLY PUBLISHED IN ULLANS NUMMER 4, SPRING 1996

When I mention the sport of curling in an Ulster context, I have to emphasise the letter 'c', not 'h' (ie curling, not hurling), as few people are aware that in the nineteenth century, and possibly before that time, outdoor curling was a pastime enjoyed in parts of Ulster. It seems to have died out just after the turn of the 20th century, with an unsuccessful attempt to revive the sport in Newtownards in 1910.

Admittedly, today there is an Irish curling team, but it comprises expatriates based 'across the water' competing in indoor ice rinks, a far cry from the frostier days of, say, the 1870s and 1890s, during the final phase of the so-called Little Ice Age (which reached its maximum development about 1750, from an estimated beginning in the thirteenth century). Indeed, there is a theory that the severe weather conditions of this Little Ice Age were a factor in leading some Lowland Scots to seek pastures new in Ulster, or to their being sent there.

Early historians of the sport of curling surmised – without quoting any evidence – that curling accompanied the settlers to Ireland during the reign of James I of England and Ireland (and VI of Scotland). This is possible, though there is no known evidence to support this claim. If the sport did cross the Irish Sea, it is said to have 'speedily died out', and it may well be that the comparative mildness of climate was unfavourable to the sport. Apart from climatic conditions, it has been suggested that the condition of the country had been unfavourable to curling, there being a lack of sympathy and cordial understanding between 'The tenant and his jolly laird, The pastor and his flock', which in Scotland made the sport so enjoyable.

The first definite evidence of curling in Ireland arose from the activities of Dr John Cairnie, of Curling Hall, Largs, Ayrshire, a great enthusiast in the development of the game. He was friendly with James Boomer of the Falls Road Flax Mill, and in 1839 encouraged him to make a curling pond (about half an acre in extent) in his grounds at Seaview, Shore Road, Belfast, and to set up a club. The club was affiliated to the Grand Caledonian Curling Club (now the Royal Caledonian Curling Club), the regulating body of the sport, in 1841-2. Boomer died in 1852 and about this time the club ceased to exist. It was revived by four gentlemen with experience of Scottish curling, who used the Thistle Tavern, Waring Street, Belfast (later in Arthur Square) as their base to set out in a search for suitable ice whenever the hard frost set in. They had, on one occasion, a problem with 'roughs', who tried to steal their belongings and another time with a 'humble cow', which trampled their ice on a pond temporarily obtained. The nomads were thus glad, eventually, to return to the Seaview pond, by courtesy of Mr Boomer's widow, who became Patroness of the club. A contemporary account described a piper accompanying the curling with renderings of 'Scotch airs, with now and then a touch of The Protestant Boys, Boyne Water etc'. In 1855, the Belfast Club seems to have reaffiliated itself to the Royal Caledonian Curling Club.

There are said to have been 'international matches' between the curling clubs of Ardrossan and Largs, and the Belfast Club 'in Ireland in the mid-1850s', though I have yet to find confirmation of this.

Curlers were certainly enthusiastic in those days. It is recorded that one Scots expatriate, in the winter of 1859, hearing of keen, gleg ice at Seaview, travelled 'one snell frosty morning' from his home at Ballyronan, County Londonderry, by gig and rail to Belfast, with his 'stanes an' kowe an' a'.

In January 1861 the Ardrossan Castle Curling Club met the Belfast Club at Seaview, after a stormy voyage across, but the match was abandoned after heavy rain intervened half-way through. A return match took place at Ardrossan on 31 December, the same year. Another game is recorded against Ardrossan at Seaview in the Royal Caledonian Curling Club Annual of 1871-2. On Boxing Day 1878, again at Seaview, a Scottish rink (a team of four curlers) from Perthshire met the Belfast Club before travelling next day to Drumbanagher Castle, near Poyntzpass, County Armagh, by invitation of the local MP, Maxwell Close Esq, for a return encounter with the Belfast rink. Three weeks later, two Ayrshire rinks travelled over to meet the Belfast Club, this time on the pond at Dunraven, Malone Road, Belfast, the residence of James P Corry Esq, MP.

During that hard winter of 1878-9, two curling clubs were founded in County Down. One with 15 ordinary members was established at Clandeboye, near Bangor, Lord Dufferin being president and active promoter. The lake in the demesne was used for the sport. Through the initiative of Mr W Sibbald Johnston, a club, initially with 40 members, was formed in late January 1879 near Mr Johnston's linen chemical bleach works, at Milecross, Kiltonga, Newtownards. They used Bradshaw's Dam (part of which still remains) and the Kiltonga Dam (in the present wild-fowl area). Sixteen pairs of curling stones were ordered by telegraph from Thomas Thorburn's Curling Stone Works at Beith in Ayrshire, when the Kiltonga Club was founded, though half of these arrived too late, as the thaw set in. The first part of the order comprised four Ailsa Craig stones, double soled, with brass mounted handles, at 46/- a pair, and four Burnock stones at 42/- a pair.

Whenever ice conditions were favourable in the following years, competitions took place between rinks from the Ulster curling clubs. Another 'international' encounter took place in May 1880 between two Belfast rinks and two from Liverpool. The late date (May) is explained by the fact that the contest was played in the indoor Southport Glaciarium, which had opened in the previous year. The year 1895 was revered by the curling community in Ulster, as several weeks of hard frost occurred in January and February. The three curling clubs occupied themselves busily. Lough Neagh froze over, and excursion trains, or trains with special fares for skaters, ran to Antrim, Glenavy, Crumlin and Toome. Although I have not yet managed to find any record in print of curling on Lough Neagh at this time, I did speak on the telephone recently to a farmer (and curler) residing near Glamis, in Perthshire, who insists that his great-grandfather took part in a 'curling international' on Lough Neagh in the 1890s and that family tradition is that a horse and cart were used to carry the stones across the ice. The year 1895 would have been the only one in the 1890s when this was possible. Incidentally, it was on a Saturday afternoon in early February 1895 that a serious tragedy was narrowly averted, when the ice gave way on the Clandeboye lake, and numerous persons fell into 15 feet of water. Skating, not curling, was taking place at the time. The year turned out to be exceptional, however, and a series of mild winters heralded the end of curling by the three Ulster clubs. The last record of actual play at Kiltonga was described in a newspaper report of 2 February 1902, of a match between the home club and the Belfast Club. During the game, a curling stone sank through the ice, and this turned out to be the club's final event. An unsuccessful attempt to relaunch the club was made in January 1910, but a rapid thaw set in. The curling stones were kept in the now-demolished Kiltonga Bleach Works, in the hope that the old-time winters would recur, and as a newspaper history of the club had it, 'maybe we shall hear the whoops and wails of the Curlers once again ring over Bradshaw's Brae'. It was, apparently, not to be. Some of the old curling stones have survived, and I know their whereabouts.

I have not been able to find out so far when curling ended at Clandeboye, but it was presumably about the same time as the demise of the other clubs. The Belfast Club remained a member of the Royal Caledonian Curling Club until 1905, but the final date of curling at the Seaview pond is not now known. The pond was subsequently filled in and built over. The house was demolished in the 1920s.

Lastly, an anecdote, which almost mirrors an event in Neil Munro's humorous dialect novel, *Fancy Farm* (1910), comes to mind. I was told of an incident during the late stages of the Kiltonga Club involving two young girls who had the task of carrying a full soup tureen down the hill for the curlers' lunch. Instead of going down the road, they took a short cut across the ice. Seeing the men skimming the stones across the frozen surface of the dam, they did the same with the warm soup tureen. But the ice melted, and the tureen went to the bottom. I wonder if it is still there to this day?

LA RUSSE

1st Figure

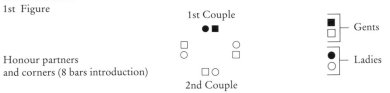

1st Couple

**Honour partners
and corners (8 bars introduction)**

2nd Couple

■ — Gents

● — Ladies

The following 8 movements are repeated 4 times until each couple in turn has taken the 'lead'
(as for 1st couple below)

(1) Swing Corners (8 bars)	
(2) Swing Partners (8 bars)	
(3) 1st couple swing on (8 bars)	
(4) 1st couple 'pass through' 2nd couple (4 bars)	
(5) Leading couple turn outwards and pass outside of second couple who are 'passing through' to original position (4 bars)	
(6) All join hands and ring round clockwise	
(7) Men centre left hands ladies on outside, 'star' round anti-clockwise	
(8) All turn about and 'star' clockwise	

Break and swing corners to repeat another 3 times until all couples have 'swung on' as in (3).

Ulster-Scots Country Dances: La Russe

by Mrs Jeannie Peak (Dance Movements)
Mr Jackie Donnan (Fiddle Music)

ORIGINALLY PUBLISHED IN ULLANS NUMMER 4, SIMMER 1996

The La Russe square dance begins, as do all these traditional square dances, in the 'quadrille' formation, as shown left. This means four couples facing each other in a small tight square (about two steps out from a centre point). The leading or first couple is always that with its back to the music at the 'top' of the room. To its left is the 4th couple, opposite the 2nd couple, and to its right is the 3rd couple. Each couple stands with gent to the left and lady on the right. Again as with all square dances, during the introductory bars of music partners turn to each other, bow (called 'honouring'), turn to the person on their other side, and bow to or honour their 'corners'. This formation of eight dancers in a square is called a 'set', and there may be as many sets as space and numbers permit.

Each traditional square dance is arranged into a number of different dances called 'figures'. In many, such as the Quadrilles, Lancers and Caledonians etc., there are five or six figures and it is customary to honour partners and corners at the beginning of each figure. However, other *oul figger dances* (as these old country dances were often called) consisted of one figure only, for example, 'Trip to the Cottage', 'Soldier's Joy', 'Bessie Black', etc.

The La Russe is unusual in that it is a relatively short dance and contains only two figures.

Unless otherwise stated, all movements in these dances are progressed by means of a simple walking step in time to the music (except of course for 'swinging' and where a 'polka' step is identified). At all times men step off with the left foot and ladies with the right.

Gowf or goff was played by all classes in Scotland.

Golf in Ulster

by Philip Robinson
ORIGINALLY PUBLISHED IN ULLANS NUMMER 6, SPRING 1998

G olf (*gowf* or *goff* in Scots) is probably the best-known Scottish traditional sport, now enjoyed by millions throughout the world. There are records of it being played in Scotland since 1457, although most of these documents refer to the breaking of the Sabbath by playing at 'the *gowf*' on Sundays (a clash of two Scottish traditions which we are still aware of today).

Until the Honourable Company of Edinburgh Golfers was established in 1744, and the Royal and Ancient Club of St Andrews in 1754, the traditional game involved hitting for distance, usually along the back of coastal sand-dunes called *links*. The oldest surviving golf club was founded by James I (of England and Scotland) in 1608 at Blackheath. James I was the monarch who initiated the Ulster Plantation, and during his reign *gowf* or *goff* was played by all classes in Scotland.

In Ulster at this time, one of James I's most important Plantation landlords was Hugh Montgomery of Newtownards. When Sir Hugh built a 'great school' at Newton in County Down, about 1630, he allowed the scholars a 'green for recreation at goff, football and archery'. Over 150 years later, in the 1780s, Sir Hugh's successor as landlord of the extensive Ards estates was Robert Stewart, Lord Castlereagh. Castlereagh was of Donegal Scottish plantation stock, and in setting out the 'Mountstewart' demesne for his new house near Greyabbey, he landscaped an area for playing golf. A portrait of Lord Castlereagh survives at Mountstewart, probably from about 1790, showing him standing with a golf club. Beside him is a golf ball on the ground. This is certainly the earliest illustration of anyone in Ulster actually playing golf.

Given the Scottish origins of the sport, it is not surprising that some of the words associated with the sport are rooted in the Scots language too.

.... LINKS ....

In the *Dictionary of the Older Scottish Tongue*, the words *linkis, lynkis, lincks* etc are defined as 'a stretch of comparatively level or gently undulating open, sandy ground having turf, bent-grass or gorse growing on it, normally near the sea-shore and commonly including sand-dunes'. The term often appears in place names, such as 'le lynkis de Leith' in 1453. Links were used for grazing, for maintaining rabbit warrens, for musters and for sports, including golf. In the *Scottish National Dictionary* (which covers the use of Scots words after 1700), the definition of *links* is:

The sandy undulating ground, generally covered with turf, bent grass, gorse, etc, which is freq. found near the sea-shore on a flat part of the coast, and is often common ground belonging to the nearest town. General Scots. Very common as a place-name associated with most sea-side burghs in Scotland.

The specific meaning of *links* as 'a golf-course' on such terrain goes back in Scots to 1728 with Allan Ramsay's *Poems*:

> Then on the Links, or in the Estler Walls,
> He drives the Gowff, or strikes the Tennis Balls.

.... TEE ....

In the *Scottish National Dictionary*, a *tee* is 'the small heap of sand or earth from which the ball is driven at the start of each hole'. Again, from Ramsay's *Poems*, we find in 1721:

> Driving their Baws frae Whins or Tee,
>   There's no ae Gowfer to be seen.
> (Driving their balls from gorse or tee,
>   There's not one Golfer to be seen).

.... DIVOT ....

For this word the *Scottish National Dictionary* has 'a turf, sod. General Scots'. This meaning is applied in Scots to all sods or tufts, with the golfing term being a recent borrowing into English from Scots.

.... FORE ....

The *Concise Scots Dictionary* notes that *fore* was used in Scots from the late nineteenth century as a shouted warning to anyone in the path of the golf ball.

Fore-caddie has been used since the late eighteenth century in Scots to describe the *caddie*, who went on ahead of the player to watch where the golf ball fell.

The following Scots meanings are also given in the *Concise Scots Dictionary*:

CADDIE:
(a) a military cadet (recorded from early seventeenth century);
(b) a messenger or errand-boy (eighteenth century);

(c) a ragamuffin, a rough lad or fellow (from late eighteenth century, now Aberdeenshire, Fife and Ulster);
(d) an attendant who carries a player's clubs in golf (from nineteenth century).

BUNKER:
(a) a bank of earth etc. at the roadside (from nineteenth century);
(b) a large heap of stones or clay (from late nineteenth century);
(c) a small sandpit, now especially on a golf-course (from nineteenth century);
(d) a storage receptacle for household coal (from eighteenth century).

PUTT (verb):
(a) push, shove; nudge gently, prod (from fifteenth century)
(b) (especially athletics), hurl a stone or heavy metal ball from the shoulder (from late sixteenth century);
(c) (golf) strike the ball with a series of gentle taps so as to move it towards the hole (from late seventeenth century).

GREEN:
(golf) the piece of finely turfed grass used as the putting ground; formerly also the fairway, or the whole course (from eighteenth century).

From the 1880s on, the popularity of the modern game of golf grew rapidly in Ulster and Scotland and spread across the world. A host of local golf links and clubs were set up in the late nineteenth century, including Royal Belfast in 1881 (at Kinnegar, Holywood) and Helen's Bay in 1896. The Royal Portrush was first formed in 1888, becoming the Royal County Club in 1892 and the Royal Portrush in 1895. Tourist guides of about 1900 often compared the Portrush links with those of St Andrews in Scotland, only just admitting that the latter alone might be superior. A more restrained description is given in *Blacks Guide Book of the North of Ireland*, which in 1912 stated that 'the Portrush Golf Links are considered the best in Ireland and equal for turf, hazards and scenery to most of the finest greens in Scotland'.

The Royal County Down, Newcastle, Golf Club was opened in 1889, getting its present name in 1910. Bangor Golf Club was opened in 1904 and was the subject of a humorous article in the *County Down Spectator* of 3 June 1904. Today, a keen interest in the game is maintained throughout Northern Ireland, supplying several first-class professionals. It might be some consolation to know, next time you are trying to hack your way out of the rough, that you are helping to perpetuate the game of your guid Scotch forebears.

Strangford Lough, Greyabbey

Some Names in the Greyabbey District

by Will McAvoy, Elspeth Barnes and Philip Robinson
ORIGINALLY PUBLISHED IN ULLANS NUMMER 1, SPRING 1993

We all can remember the names we used for our childhood haunts, not always knowing what the names meant or how old they were. What is often special about these is that they have been handed down from generation to generation by word of mouth. If they are not recorded now, many will be lost forever, for they are not the names one will find on official maps or in legal documents like leases.

One type of place name that hasn't been attracting much attention from historians is local field names. Over the past few years, Will McAvoy has been gathering field names from farms around the village of Greyabbey in the Ards Peninsula, County Down. Starting around Mid Island (where his own family had farmed for generations), he recruited a few friends and moved on to neighbours' farms in the townlands of Ballyurnanellan, Kilnatierny, Gordonnall, Mountstewart, Ballymurphy, Ballyboley, Ballynester, Ballyboghilbo and Blackabbey.

At the end of this exercise hundreds of local place names had been collected and written down for the first time. Of field names alone, almost 250 were mapped. This article will give readers some idea of the sorts of names still used locally, and how much interesting information can be gleaned from a small area.

FIEL, FIELD (pronounced *feel* locally and usually written as *fiel* in Scots)
Less than half of all the field names collected – only 88 in fact – had the word *field* or *fiel* in them. Most of these had another word to do with farming: 19, for example, had the surname of a previous owner (Caughey's Fiel, Corry's Fiel, Carson's Fiel, Askin's Fiel, Blair's Fiel, Gibson's Fiel, Taggart's Fiel, Patterson's Fiel, Jackson's Fiel, etc.) or both the Christian name and the surname (Andy Carson's Fiel, Tom Keags' Fiel, Willie Morrison's Fiel, Tom Regan's Fiel, Old Jimmy Katie's Fiel, James's Fiel, Robin Davidson's Fiel, etc.) These folk are hardly remembered today, and one field, Betsy Gray's Fiel, is named for a heroine of the 1798 rebellion! There were 7 Well Fiels, two Stable Fiels, two Byre (cow-house) Fiels, two Lint-Hole (flax-dam) Fiels, a Hen-House Fiel, a Kill (kiln) Fiel, a Plantin (tree plantation or wood) Fiel, a Car House (cart-shed) Fiel, a Stile Fiel, a Peat-Stack Fiel, a Stack-Yard Fiel, a Yard Fiel, a Stack-Garden Fiel and a Bullock Fiel.

There were three Fitba (football) Fiels, a Milestone Fiel, a Spring Fiel, a Breek (brick) Fiel and a number of fields named after the type of land: a Clay-Hole Fiel, a Garden Fiel, a Bog Fiel, a Rocky Fiel and a Gravelly Fiel. The shape or size of the field was sometimes described in the names, with four Wee Fiels, two Long Fiels, a Point Fiel and a Hatchet Fiel. (This last is L-shaped, like an axe).

The whereabouts of the field can be part of the name too, and we have three Low Fiels, two Upper Fiels, a Front Fiel, a Back Fiel, a Middle Fiel, and a Shore Fiel. As well as these short names, some were known only by longer titles, such as the Fiel Fornent The Door, the Fiel at the Back o the Plantin, or the Fiel on the Low Side o the Loanen (lane). Only in two of the ten townlands covered (Ballyurnanellan and Kilnatierny) did the majority of the field names include the word *fiel*. These two townlands run on to the Strangford Lough shore and have a good deal of flat, coastal land in them. Because names with *fiel* were more common on this land, which seems to have been more recently enclosed into fields, it may be that they are generally 'younger' names than the rest.

HILL (pronounced *hal*)

Fields using the word *hill* were the second biggest group recorded, with 62 field names containing the word. These fields do not contain a whole hill, in the English sense, but are fields on a slope. For example, there was a field at the bottom end of a hill called the Bottom Hill and the one above it called the Top Hill. The fields on the long ridge running along the north of Greyabbey Main Street were known as The Hills, but there was only one hill there. In Ulster-Scots a roadside house that 'sits on a steep hill' is not at the top of the hill, but is built on a steep slope (or brae). The large number of these names is hardly surprising in the middle of County Down's drumlin country, and the labouring of these fields sometimes meant that soil had crept down the hill and had to be carted back to the top of the field. This is sometimes given to explain that the horse-drawn 'Scotch carts' used were nearly always 'coupin' carts with a tipping release mechanism.

As far as fields with *hill* were concerned, many of these had part of their name used to indicate their place. There were four Front Hills, four Back Hills, a Back Hill Facing the Road, a Wee Back Hill, a Near Back Hill and a Far Back Hill. There were three Middle Hills, one Far Hill, two Top Hills, two Bottom Hills, along with a Plantin Hill, a Tough Hill and a Hill at the Shore. There were again many Hills with personal names: Dorey's Hill, Pat's Hill, Lawry's Hill, Andy's Hill, M'Cance's Hill, Billie's Hill, Boyd's Hill, Annett's Hill, Sloan's Hill, Loughin's Hill and Carson's Hill.

Other features included three Well Hills, a Forth (ring-fort or rath) Hill, a Stile Hill, a Shepherd's Hill, a Smiddy Hill, a Spring Hill, a Quarry Hill, a Stable Hill, a Horse Hill, a Barley Hill, a Kill Hill, two Cottage Hills, a Round Hill, a Priest's Hill, a Doctor's Hill, a Church Hill, and a Rectory Hill. In Ballyboley there was a Back Kearney Hill and a Near Kearney Hill.

BRAE
Only two field names used the Scots word meaning slope (*brae*) rather than *hill*. These were Burn (stream) Brae in Ballyboley and Hangin Brae in Ballymurphy. The second of these marks the location of the execution of Rev James Porter in 1798. Porter was the Presbyterian minister in Greyabbey who was hanged on suspicion of support for the United Irishmen. It might have been expected that Brae would have been in more common use here for field names, given the large number of Hill fields. Brae is still in common use as a general term for any slope, and some road and laneways have particular names such as the Meetin House Brac in Greyabbey and Muckleboy Brae on the Ballymurphy Road. Muckleboy was the original spelling of the family name used by the present McAvoys in this locality (including Will McAvoy, the collector of these names), and is recorded as such in the 1868 Griffith Valuation. As late as 1901, the Census Enumerators Returns for Mid Island were spelling Will's grandfather's family all as McIlboys.

BOG (pronounced *boag* or *boge*)
There are no fields in this area that contain workable peat. A peat bog is called a moss here. Fields with the name Bog in them are simply marshes or poorly drained fields. The 18 Bog field names include Sam's Bog, Tam's Bog, Billie's Bog, Caughey's Bog, Robert's Bog, Matthew's Bog, Sam Wright's Bog, Askin's Long Bog and Askin's Near Bog. There are two Far Bogs, a Long Bog, a Near Bog, a Wee Bog, a Mair (rough land) Bog and three fields simply known as The Bog or The Bogs.

MAIRS (pronounced *mares*)
Mair (or muir) is a Scotch word meaning 'rough, uncultivated land'. As well as the Mair Bog mentioned above, one field in Ballymurphy is called James Brown's Mairs.

KNOWES (pronounced *nows*, not *knows*)
This Scots word means 'a knoll' and is usually used in the plural to mean a hummocky, rough field. Of the 15 Knowe field names collected, only one (the Wee Knowe) does not give the plural Knowes. There are four fields simply called The Knowes, and five with personal names: Hall's Knowes, Edgar's Knowes, Frank's Knowes, Katie's Knowes, and Taggart's Knowes. Other fields include two Back Knowes, an Old Knowes, a Young Knowes, and a Well Knowes.

ACRE

A dozen names were collected that end in Acre. Only one, Matthew's Acre, indicated anything other than the size of the field, eg Nine Acre. There is one Four Acre, three Five Acres, a Six Acre, two Seven Acres, an Eight Acre, a Nine Acre, a Ten Acre and a Twelve Acre. Acres (in the plural) is never used. The actual measurement is Cunningham Measure – for example, the Seven Acre in Black Abbey contains 9 statute acres. Obviously, the numerals are (or were formerly) pronounced in the Scots forms, and the names run together to give 'senagher' (Seven Acre), 'echtagher' (Eight Acre), etc.

GARDEN

The four fields named Gardens were not domestic gardens in the model sense, although one, M'Kays Garden, may be named to mark the site of an abandoned homestead. The Long Garden and the Back Garden were small fields which had been laboured with the spade, and the Sally Garden was a small field in Ballymurphy used to grow osiers or willows ('sally rods') for basket-making and thatching.

LAND, LAN, LAUN (pronounced *lawn*)

Only three fields were called Land, one a field called the Rough Lan in Ballymurphy, and the others (in Ballyboley and Black Abbey) were called Black Lan. Here black is not a colour, but like black mouth, black potatoes, blackguard, black house and black-hearted means 'bad or inferior' (ground). (Of course the townland name of Black Abbey was different. It was the site of a medieval monastery where the monks wore black habits.)

GROUND, GROUN (pronounced *groon* or *grun*): One field in Ballyurnanellan is called the Sandy Groun, and another in Ballymurphy was the Rough Groun.

PARK: One field in Gordonnall is called the Hill Park.

MEADOW (pronounced *meeda*): One field in Gordonnall is called Shanners's Meadow.

BAY: Two fields at the shore in Mountstewart are called Watering Bay and Bar Bay.

GLEN: Two fields in Ballymurphy are called The Glen.

COMMONS: One field in Ballyboley is called The Common.

The following table shows how many of the different types of basic names given to fields were found in each townland.

Townland	'field'	'hill'	'bog'	'knowes'	'acre'	'garden'	'land'
Ballyboley	31	12	8	3	5		1
Ballymurphy	6	18	1	7		3	1
Ballynester	11	3	4	3	1		
Black Abbey	1	3			1		
Ballyboghilbo	4	5	5	1			
Greyabbey	14	10					
Ballyurnanellan	9	3					
Gordonnall	1	2			5		
Kilnatierny	10	2		1		1	
Mount Stewart	1	4					
Total:	88	62	18	15	12	4	2

This table does not include the types of field names for which only one or two examples are found, such as Ground, Common, etc. However, there are about 50 or so field names that didn't use any of these terms. Some of these don't need an explanation, like The Orchard (although in both of the two examples gathered there is no orchard there today), The Quarries, and so on. The following list contains some of the most interesting ones.

THE DIPPER: A field in Ballymurphy where sheep were dipped.

THE ISLE: This is a common place name in the Ards for hilly ground surrounded by bogs or marshy land. We found it used only once as a field name.

THE PUN: A field near Greyabbey village on the shore had the 'pound' for livestock when markets were held there. Greyabbey was granted a charter for a weekly market in 1605, but there is no record of markets being held for several centuries back.

THE FORTH: Forth is the common name for a rath or circular earthen 'fort' of the Early Christian Period.

THE KIRKS: This name was given to a field in Black Abbey townland that was the site of the medieval abbey. There was no trace of the building by the twentieth century.

BOG ONION: A field in Ballyboley. Its meaning is unknown.

FAR DRUSHEY/NEAR DRUSHEY: These two fields in Ballyboley may be the only examples with a Gaelic origin. *Dris* (pronounced DREESH) in Irish means a wild briar or bramble.

THE NACKIES: The meaning of this name of a field in Ballyboley is unknown, although the Scots word *knackie* means 'handy' or 'clever'.

THE LONG SHOT: This is a field in Ballyurnanellan. There is another Long Shot in the demesne of Rosemount House at Greyabbey. Here the name is said to have come from soldiers or yeomanry using the open area as target practice. This long field at Rosemount was once the old line of the main Portaferry Road (before 1800), and some 'long shots' are thought to have been straight stretches of road where men playing road bowls or 'bullets' could get a clear throw.

THE FREEHOUL: A field in Black Abbey, presumably one that had been held in 'freehold' rather than on lease by what were tenant-farmers up until about 1900.

Almost all of the several hundred field names collected around Greyabbey had never been written down before. However, when collecting these and talking about them among members of Greyabbey and District Historical Society, it was obvious that there was a host of other interesting place names in the district other than those given to fields.

Starting with our own village, Greba or Grayba (pronounced *Graiba*) is the local name for Greyabbey, and it has been written as Greba by local poets and other Ulster-Scots writers for well over 150 years. Inside Greyabbey, the official names of the streets are not necessarily the same as those used. North Street is (or was) Hard Breid Raa (after oatcakes, the common fare of residents there); Main Street (at the top end) was the Big Raa; Church Street was Water Lane; and the Meetin-Hoose Brae is where the Newton (Newtownards) Road comes into Main Street. This junction, at the Kosy Korner, formerly Buntin's Corner, is opposite the police barracks, beside the site of the old weigh-brig. The Meetin-Hoose Brae was a new line for the Newtownards-Portaferry Road, opened some time before 1800, and later a deeper cut was made to lessen the slope of the brae. Material from the cut was dumped on the Strangford Lough shore by a contractor called Gill, and so the new ground there became known as Gill's Isle, beside another piece of ground on the foreshore called Goat Isle. The original line of the through road is still identified by a narrow lane marked with a sign for School Lane. This is also known as Sammy Brown's Loanen or the Schule Loanen; before 1830 it went straight on through the present gates to Rosemount House, along the Lang

Shot. Beside this is a raised earthen rath (known as The Moat) although it is nearly obscured by the trees of the Plantin, overlooking the Shore Road to Portaferry, which was built about 1820 around a small bay. The fresh-water lake formed in this inlet, Greyabbey Lake to give it its proper name, is known by some Kirkcubbin folk as the Swan Hole.

All these names are found at the shore (or low) end of the Main Street, with the Abbey ruins at the top end. Moving up Main Street, three small loanens on the left, two of them named after the owners of the fields to which they give access, run between the houses. One is known as Dunn's Loanen and another as Davy Davison's Loanen. A vacant site (once used for bonfires) on the other side is called The Meeda, and behind this a stream (simply known as The Burn) separates the village from the demesne lands of Rosemount House. The Burn, just before it enters the outside of the village from the east, drops quickly over a stony bed and so is known there as the Rummlin Roaks.

One terrace of two-storey houses along the Big Raa is called Askin's Raa. Turning left at the head of Main Street is Hard Breid Raa, with Andy Carson's Loanen off to one side and the Smiddy Hill behind the houses on the other side. The bottom slope of Smiddy Hill is the Gressie Gairdens, and at the top of Hard Breid Raa the road out of the village forks. One road here goes towards Carrowdore, and although it is officially called the Carrowdore Road, it is known locally as the Ballyboley Road. One of the first hills along this road is Muckleboy's Brae, named after the McAvoys that lived there. On the Newton Road is the Pea Hill Brae, named after a field called the Pea Hill or Plea Hill.

One very localised feature of pronunciation introduces an 'r' where it would not be expected. 'Out and about' and 'spoutings' (gutters) can become *ort an abort* and *spurtins*. So too 'loanen' can become *lornen*. Around Greyabbey, countless scores of lanes are known by local names, such as the Lang Loanen, the Doctor's Loanen and so on. Signs for the major roads are a fairly recent innovation, dating from the replacement of townland names some years ago by road names for postal addresses, a shift giving rise to the Save Our Townland campaign, which is still active. The signs by no means always have the same names as those used locally. The Quarry Road, for example, is more often known as the Bugglebo Road.

The townlands around Greyabbey, working in a clockwise direction from the Strangford Lough shore to the north, are Ballyurnanellan, Kilnatierney, Gordonnall, Ballymurphy, Ballynester, Tullykevin, Ballyboghilbo and (back to the lough shore south of Rosemount townland), Ballybryan and The Bootown. Some readers will be aware that Volume II of *Place-Names of Northern Ireland* (for the Ards) was published in 1992. This fine work of Celtic scholarship provides the Gaelic meaning of these townland names. Ballyurnanellan is explained as 'the townland of the yew of the island', where *ellan* (a Norse-influenced form of *island*) is used rather than the more usual Gaelic *inis*. Last century it was suggested by O'Donovan in his *Ordnance Survey Name Book* of the 1840s that the name meant 'townland of the arable land belonging to the island', or 'at the edge of the island', presumably because of the adjacent Mid and South Isles in Strangford Lough.

Gordonnall is noted as 'of uncertain origin' in the 1992 study, noting that O'Donovan's explanation of it as Gort Donnell ('Donnell's Garden') does not rest well with the local pronunciation, where the stress is on the last rather than the first syllable – something like 'Gor-don-ALL', not 'Gor-DON-all'. Local tradition in Greyabbey maintains that this townland was a land gift from the Montgomerys to a family called Gordon in service at Rosemount House. Indeed, one local sampler dated 1864 has 'Gordon Hall' embroidered at the base.

Kilnatierney is 'the Lord's little wood', or (according to O'Donovan) 'St Tierney's church'. The older spelling (Callnaterny) is close to the local pronunciation.

Tullykevin is 'Kevin's hillock', although the usual local pronunciation of the name (*Tullycavey*) is not recorded.

Ballymurphy is 'Murphy's townland', and Ballyboghilbo 'the townland of the cowherd'. For the second of these townlands, which is situated between the ruins of the medieval Grey Abbey and the deserted site of Black Abbey, the local pronunciation *Bugglebo* is correctly recorded, although the authors of the 1992 volume seem unaware of the Scots word *boglebo* 'spectre, ghost'. One nineteenth-century local poet (who always referred to Greyabbey as Greba) even wrote a poem called 'Bugglebo' about ghosts and demons.

Ballybryan (pronounced locally *Bally-BRAIN*) is sometimes spelt Ballybrane on headstones in the grave-yard, and The Bootown (pronounced *BOOT-n*) is a Norse/Old English place name derived from Old Norse *bu* meaning 'farm' or 'dwelling'.

Although the Gaelic explanation of Ballynester as from *Baile an Aistire* or 'the townland of the doorkeeper' is certainly more plausible than O'Donovan's 'Nester's townland', the Old Norse word *nestr* 'provisions' is perhaps also worthy of consideration. Rosemount, the townland containing the demesne land of Rosemount or Greyabbey House, has been the seat of the Montgomery family since the 1630s (when it was first named Montrose).

Other place names around Greyabbey mentioned in the recent volume include a few other local names which are not Gaelic in origin. Haw Hill, for example, is incorrectly identified in the survey as being named from the Scots word *haw* 'hawthorn', when it is in fact from another Scots word, *ha* or *haw* meaning 'hall' or 'big house'.

Elsewhere in the vicinity of the village we have Blackwood's Plantin, a wooded area originally on the Clandeboy estate (the family name of the Clandeboys was Blackwood during the late 1700s). The woods of the Rosemount estate are simply called The Plantin, and a wooded area beside Mid Isle at the lough shore is Skillen's Plantin.

Several islands in Strangford Lough lie off Greyabbey and are included in Greyabbey Parish. These include Mid Isle, South Isle, Chapel Isle, The Chanderies, Boretree Island, Boretree Rock, Gabbock Isle, Hare Isle, Peggy's Isle, Pig Isle, Turley Rock and Whaup Rock. The English meaning of many of these is self-evident, and several have Scots meanings such as *whaup* ('curlew'), *gabbock* ('dog-fish') or *channerie* ('gravelly'). Some of these Scots words are in turn derived from Norse, and in Strangford they might even be Norse or Viking survivals. The *-ey* ending found in so many Strangford island names (such as Turley Rock) may well signal the Norse *ey*, meaning 'island', as in *sker-ey* (*skerries* 'rock islands') and *plad-ey* (*pladdys* 'flat/plate islands').

Boretree Island is locally believed to be named after the *bore tree* (Scots for 'elder tree'), but it was suggested in 1925 by D E Lowry that this was in fact a corruption of the Norse *bortr-ey* 'distant or far away Isles'. The Boretrees are the furthest islands up into Strangford from a Viking (ie sea-based) point of view.

South Isle is connected to Mid Isle, and Mid Isle to the mainland by natural shingle causeways called The Roans. The origin of this Ulster-Scots word is obscure, but it may indicate the back-to-back 'row-ends', that is, the high tide beach marks of seaweed called *rows* in Scots (perhaps from the 'rolls' of seaweed marking this point). Alternatively, and more probably, the name may just be a Scots word of Scandinavian origin *roan* meaning 'a thicket of bushes', as there is such on the landward side.

There are, in addition, numerous local names given to less obvious features of the shore and countryside around Greyabbey. When all these place names are added to the lengthy list of local field names collected for the same district, an enormous wealth of Ulster-Scots place names can be gleaned from a relatively small area. Surely, then, the same wealth of unrecorded Ulster-Scots place names must exist throughout much of the Ulster countryside.

We would like to thank all the local folk that helped with this survey: in particular Miss Millen, Tommy M'Avoy, Eddie Muckle, Hugh Dorrian, Ivan Brown, Ernie Hall and Herbie Carson.

Ever thocht o a career in this Ulster-Scots business?

A Test for Ulster-Scots

by Philip Robinson
ORIGINALLY PUBLISHED IN ULLANS NUMMER 6, SPRING 1998

Ulster-Scots is often confused with Ulster 'dialect' for a very good reason: Ulster-English dialect contains many Scots words and pronunciations when compared to the English spoken in England or the south of Ireland. From outside, all Ulster speech can sound very Scottish, particularly the 'accent' in Antrim, Down, Londonderry and Donegal. Ulster-Scots, however, is more than Ulster dialect. It is a living version of the Lowland Scots language which has recognition as a traditional, regional language of Europe.

How then can we tell the difference between somebody who is talking Ulster-Scots and somebody who is using Ulster-English dialect? The easiest way to identify Ulster-Scots is by listening for a number of 'speech markers'. These are the most common words used by Ulster-Scots speakers and not by speakers of Ulster English. For example, the Scots words *thon, dander* and *wee* ('that', 'stroll', and 'little') are used every day by the great majority of folk throughout Ulster. Although they are Scots rather than English words, they have simply been borrowed into Ulster-English dialect.

On the other hand, words like *nicht, cannae* and *gye* ('night', 'can't' and 'very') are very common markers of Ulster-Scots speech. They are also markers of Ulster-Scots literature, if one wishes to distinguish this from Ulster-English 'dialect' writing.

It is important to remember that almost all Ulster-Scots speakers will use the markers only in each other's company. When speaking to an outsider, in public, or to a professional person such as a teacher, minister or doctor, Ulster-Scots speakers will switch to Standard English, or – more often – to Ulster-English dialect, which is regarded as more acceptable.

The following list of 67 everyday words shows how English, Ulster-English dialect and Ulster-Scots are different from each other. In particular, note how the first 22 are Scots words used in everyday speech throughout Ulster. The rest identify words used only in Ulster-Scots. These last 45 words can be used as markers of Ulster-Scots speech and literature. If, for example, you often hear (and sometimes use) less than 20 of this entire list, your experience of Ulster-Scots is very limited. If, however, you often hear and sometimes use more than half (33) of the words on this list, you are already part of the Ulster-Scots speaking community.

Test yourself against these scores:

0 - 11	Ye cud dae wi a bit mair lairnin!
12 - 22	Limited Ulster-Scots, mostly Ulster-English dialect
23 - 33	You can call yourself an Ulster-Scots speaker.
34 - 50	You are very familiar with current, everyday Ulster-Scots.
above 50	Ever thocht o a career in this Ulster-Scots business?

	English	Ulster-English Dialect	Ulster-Scots
1	of	o	o
2	yes	ay	ay
3	no	na	na
4	remember	min(d)	min(d)
5	small	wee	wee
6	that	thon	thon
7	stroll	dander	danner
8	today	the day	the day
9	tomorrow	the morra	the morra
10	with	wi	wi
11	lane	loanen	loanen
12	path	pad	pad
13	yonder, over there	thonder	thonder
14	to	til	til
15	ditch	sheuch	sheuch
16	brat	skitter	skitter
17	shout	gulder	gulder
18	tip over	coup	coup
19	sly	sleekit	sleekit
20	than	nor	nor
21	endure	thole	thole
22	awkward	thran	thran
23	have	have	hae
24	give	give	gie
25	not	nat	no
26	from	from	frae, fae

	English	Ulster-English Dialect	Ulster-Scots
27	any	any	onie
28	several	lock	wheen
29	stone	stone	stane
30	more	more	mair
31	most	most	maist
32	home	home	hame
33	sore	sore	sair
34	head	head	heid
35	round	roun'	roon
36	house	house	hoose
37	town	town	toon
38	foot	fut	fit
39	none	noan	nane
40	over	over	owre
41	couldn't	cud'n	cudnae
42	wouldn't	wud'n	wudnae
43	won't	won't	winnae
44	haven't	have'n	hinnae
45	can't	can't	cannae
46	one	wan	yin
47	two	two	twa
48	eight	eight	echt
49	bright	bright	bricht
50	light	light	licht
51	tonight	the night	the nicht
52	away	away	awa
53	always	aaways	aye
54	leave	lave	lee
55	sometimes	betimes	whiles
56	cow	cow	coo
57	cattle	kyattle	kye
58	very	very	gye
59	gave	give	gien
60	must	must	maun
61	mustn't	mustn't	maunnae

	English	Ulster-English Dialect	Ulster-Scots
62	anything	anythin'	ocht
63	at all	at all	ava
64	eye	eye	ee
65	eyes	eyes	een
66	go	go	gan
67	wipe	skiff	dicht

Cunningburn (between Newtownards and Greyabbey)

Ulster-Scots as Manifest in Place Names

93

by David Polley
ORIGINALLY PUBLISHED IN ULLANS NUMMER 7, WUNTER 1999

HISTORICAL PLACE NAMES

As different languages ebb and flow across the landscape, their vocabularies are used to describe places and features. These words, once merely descriptive, become proper nouns and thus achieve an independence from the fate of the language itself. We can talk about 'an archaeology' of names – different layers of names laid down at different times – and by excavating these we can begin to understand something of how people used to speak. Thus if a language is in retreat across a territory, there will still be names left behind locked in the linguistic landscape and recorded on maps. Although Gaelic has received most attention, being found across the entire island of Ireland, Ulster-Scots has also left a trace in our nomenclature. As with all such names, this can be understood to occur at three different levels.

OFFICIAL NAMES

These are legal names such as parish names and especially townland names. Kirkinriola ('Riola's Church') in County Antrim is perhaps the only definite parish name showing Ulster-Scots influence. *Kirk* is a Lowland Scots and northern English word, derived from Old Norse *kirkja*, corresponding to Old English *circe*, which gives modern *church*. Townland names are more numerous: Black Brae in County Londonderry (a *brae* is a slope often, but not always, near water), Cunningburn in County Down (*burn* is so commonly used for stream in Scots areas that it is barely thought of as unusual), and perhaps even Glar in County Donegal (*glar* is soft mud and this is a townland reclaimed from the sea).

RECORDED LOCAL NAMES

Many other names are recorded in official sources, although they have no legal importance. There are many such names on the Ordnance Survey six-inch maps, while others are recorded in the Ordnance Survey name books, although they were not chosen for inclusion on the final copies. Distribution maps of common Scots words such as *burn*, or *moss* (meaning 'peat bog'), could show where these words were of important local currency in the early nineteenth century.

UNRECORDED LOCAL NAMES

The whole country is covered with quite a mind-boggling wealth of local names and associated folk tales. Although little research has been published at this level, that which is available indicates the diversity and amount of potential material. Indeed, one entire book contains information about a single townland in the Galway Gaeltacht [1]. Another writer has pointed out the importance of local names in local history [2], although neither of these publications deals with specifically linguistic issues. Elsewhere in this book is an article on local place names around Greyabbey, and the Northern Ireland Placenames Project has recently completed a survey in East Antrim and Portaferry. In the near future we should be able to assemble a thorough range of sources for all of Ulster and begin to examine the distribution of words such as *roddin* 'grass lane', *holme* 'flat land by a river' or *march* 'farm boundary'.

Using a combination of distribution maps of various name elements at the three different scales of official, recorded local and unrecorded local names, we should be able to gain insights into the linguistic influence of Ulster-Scots throughout history. In addition, we can record names which might otherwise be lost and empower people to realise the value of their local language and traditions. Perhaps most important of all, we can contribute to the debates regarding Irish place names and work with Gaelic scholars to show the true diversity of our common heritage on this island. Many place names have a variety of possible meanings; the previously mentioned form *kirk* is also thought to be present as a surname and as a modification of *cearc*, the Gaelic word meaning 'hen' or 'moorhen'.

MODERN PLACE NAMES

Recently there has been an upsurge of interest in Ulster-Scots place names linked to government legislation allowing bilingual street signs. The sort of research mentioned before will be invaluable in this respect, as we can provide real, organic Scots names for roads now built up and renamed. For example, Brunswick Road in Bangor was previously known as Ash Loanen. I believe that encouraging such historical names to reappear is preferable to the translation of current English names. Of course, many recent housing developments are not on historical routes, in which case we could use field names or other local names as Ulster-Scots versions for these streets. Surely only as a last resort should we translate English into Scots, although in many long-developed areas this may be unavoidable. An additional advantage to using historical names is that it is less difficult to have heritage signs erected than bilingual signs, thereby speeding the increased visibility for the language which road signs achieve.

Perhaps more important, however, is our chance, through the promotion of Ulster-Scots, to encourage new developments in Scots areas to be called by Ulster-Scots names. Since many councils have announced that they are trying to use more traditional and locally resonant names in new developments, we can surely look forward to a marked increase in Scots in our built environment.

[1] S Cathain and P O'Flanagan, *The Living Landscape* (Dublin: Comhairle Bhéaloideas Éireann, 1975)
[2] A J Malley, The recording and study of field names', *Journal of Federation of Ulster Local Studies*, Vol. 3, no.1 (November, 1977)

This letter is remarkable in its language.

An Early Letter in Ulster Scots

by Michael Montgomery
ORIGINALLY PUBLISHED IN ULLANS NUMMER 2, SPRING 1994

O n deposit at the London School of Economics is one of the more unusual and diverse collections of correspondence in the British Isles – letters written home by eighteenth- and nineteenth-century English, Scottish, and Irish emigrants who went to North America. Gathered over many years by Professor Charlotte Erickson (a historian now retired from Cambridge University) when she was on the faculty at the LSE, these are designated the 'Letters from Emigrants to America' collection in the archives there. Among the oldest of the 180-odd items is the photocopy of a manuscript dated March 18, 1767, signed by a Mr James Murray of New York and addressed to a Reverend Baptist Boyd of Aughnacloy, County Tyrone. This letter is remarkable in its language and its unqualified description of the colonies as a true promised land (Murray refers Boyd to the description of Canaan in the eighth chapter of Deuteronomy and says the land around him in New York is 'far better'). Saying he is 'Clark till York Meeting House', Murray extols the land and economic opportunities available to any who would emigrate and settle there, and he implores Boyd to encourage Murray's parents, siblings, and friends to come. Full of idiosyncratic and phonetic spellings, the letter's flamboyant rhetoric and vivid imagery beg it to be read aloud. Its unusually vernacular language and early date make it of great interest to linguists; in these qualities, as well as in length and degree of detail, the letter is quite different from others written by Ulster emigrants from the period that have survived.

However, the photocopy of the Murray letter is not of an original. A reader should become suspicious when, in the middle of the third page, Murray writes, 'Now this is the last of sax [ie six] Sheets of Paper I hae written to you'. Unknown to Professor Erickson and to the LSE archives staff, the letter (more accurately, a variant of it) was published thirty years before, as the lead item in Benjamin Franklin's newspaper, the *Pennsylvania Gazette* (issue 464, October 27 - November 3, 1737) in Philadelphia. This earlier version itself had no date, and a manuscript original for it is not known, although the newspaper's preface to the letter claims the existence of one.

How many versions of the letter might there have been? Why was it written and why was it revised? The 1737 and 1767 versions are quite similar in content and sentence structure, but have innumerable differences in spelling, word form, capitalization, and punctuation. For instance, the wording in the earlier letter 'yence mere my kind Love till yer sel, Reverend Mr. Baptist Boyd' is rephrased 'ance mair to yere ane sell Reverand Doctor Baptiste Boyd' in the later one. Evidently the letter had a life of its own and was copied and altered at least once and quite possibly more often. Perhaps it passed into local folk tradition as a nostalgia piece read for the reminiscence it brought of earlier days of emigration; more likely it functioned as a propaganda statement to stimulate emigration, used by shipping agents and other parties. It is so unusual in style and so full of unconventional spellings that one might question why it was written in this form at all. Doubtless we will never know most of its history, nor have answers to most of our questions about it.

The two versions are reproduced in their entirety below. Could the one published in 1737 have been an authentic letter? Or was it fabricated by someone (maybe Franklin himself) who knew early Ulster emigrants well and who wanted to caricature their language, promote their further emigration, or both? Can the earlier version have reflected the circumstances and speech of a man named James Murray who lived in New York? So far as this writer can determine, there is no historical record either of a man by the name emigrating from County Tyrone or of a John Pemberton ('Minister of the Gospel in New-York'), to whom Murray requests that letters for him be sent.[1]

Intriguingly, however, there is evidence of a Reverend Baptist Boyd, who was alive and apparently preaching in Aughnacloy at the time of the earlier version but not the later one. According to *A History of Congregations in the Presbyterian Church in Ireland 1610-1982* [2],

> During the ministry ... of Rev. Baptist Boyd, Aghalow begins
> to break up, and the name disappears from the records. He had
> been born at Carrickfergus and was ordained on 19 Apr. 1698.
> During his career he is referred to as the minister of 'Aghaloo',
> of 'Aughnacloy', and of 'Aughnacloy and Ballygawley'. By the
> time of his death on 25 Nov. 1749, both the name and the old
> church ceased to be used.

So there is at least some historical basis to the letters. Next comes the question of the authenticity of their language. They are clearly written in some kind of Scots, featuring trademark Scotticisms like *bonny, weans, ken* and *braw*, along with numerous grammatical usages and pronunciations. But do they reflect accurately what we know about the Ulster-Scots tongue? This writer (an American linguist who is not a speaker of Ulster Scots) will make a few observations here. Readers are invited to study the letters and to decide for themselves how accurately they render Ulster usage and pronunciation. A very important point to bear in mind is that there was no tradition of writing in such broad vernacular at the time that could have served as a model. The unusual spellings in these two letters are either phonetic or semi-phonetic forms or are other creations of its author; they are not copied from other sources.

1. The 1737 version uses the Scots forms *grund*, *hund*, and *pund*, while the 1767 one uses English equivalents *ground* and *pound*.

2. The 1737 version uses *yen* (*any yen*, etc.) for 'one', the later letter only *ane* (*oney ane*, etc.).

3. The 1737 letter is more consistent, though not entirely so, in the usage of traditional Scots. For example, it tends to use *till* and *ane* before words beginning with a vowel or vowel-like sound, but *to* and *a* before consonants. The 1767 letter uses *till* and *ane* less discriminately. Similar evidence comes from the marking of concord between subjects and verbs; the traditional rule in Scots is to use *is* or mark a plural verb with the suffix -s if its subject is a noun ('There *is* Servants *comes* here out of Ereland …'). This is followed in 7/16 cases in the 1737 letter, but in only 2/12 in the later one.

Many other comparisons can be made. Here are the complete texts.

(1737 Version)
Preface and Text of James Murray of New York to Rev. Baptist Boyd of County Tyrone, Ireland (Published in the Pennsylvania Gazette, 1737)

The following Letter is said to have been sent from a Person settled in New-York, to his Countrymen, to encourage them to come over thither; which, that it might have the better Effect on the People, was printed and dispers'd in Ireland. A Copy of which being brought over, in one of the late Ships, We present our Readers with it.

A LETTER from James Murray, Thus directed; For the Kingdom of Ereland, in the North of Ereland, near to Aughnacloy, in the County of Tyrone, To Baptist Boyd, the Reverend Minister of the Gospel, in the Parish of Aughelow. Let aw Persons that see this, tak Care to send it to the Reverend Baptist Boyd, Minister of the Gospel, in the Parish of Aughelow, in the County of Tyrone, living near Aughnacloy. With Care.

Reverend Baptist Boyd,
Read this Letter, and look, and tell aw the poor Folk of your Place, that God has open'd a Door for their Deliverance; for here is ne Scant of Breed here, and if your Sons Samuel and James Boyd wad but come here, they wad get mere Money in ane Year for teechin a Letin Skulle, nor ye yer sell wad get for Three Years Preeching whar ye are. Reverend Baptist Boyd, there ged ane wee me in the Shep, that now gets ane Hundred

Punds for ane Year for teechin a Letin Skulle, and God kens, little he is skill'd in Learning, and yet they think him a high learned Man: Ye ken I had but sma Learning when I left ye, and now wad ye think it, I hea 20 Pund a Year for being a Clark to York Meeting-House, and I keep a Skulle for wee Weans: Ah dear Sir, there is braw Living in this same York for high learned Men: The young Foke in Ereland are aw but a Pack of Couards, for I will tell ye in short, this is a bonny Country, and aw Things grows here that ever I did see grow in Ereland; and wee hea Cows and Sheep, and Horses plenty here, and Goats, and Deers, and Racoons, and Moles, and Bevers, and Fish, and Fouls of aw Sorts: Trades are aw gud here, a Wabster gets 12 Pence a Yeard, a Labourer gets 4 Shillings and 6 Pence a Day, a Lass gets 4 Shillings and 6 Pence a Week for spinning on the wee Wheel, a Carpenter gets 6 Shillings a Day, and a Tailor gets 20 Shillings for making a Suit of Cleaths, a Wheel-wright gets 16 Shillings for making Lint Wheels a piece, Indian Corn, a Man wull get a Bushell of it for his Day's Work here; Rye grows here, and Oats, and Wheet, and Winter Barley, and Summer Barley; Buck Wheet grows here, na every Thing grows here. – Now I beg of ye aw to come our here, and bring our wee ye aw the Cleaths ye can of every Sort, beth o' Linen and Woollen, and Guns, and Pooder, and Shot, and aw Sorts of Weers that is made of Iron and Steel, and aw Tradesmen that comes here, let them bring their Tools wee them, and Farmers their Plough Erons; a Mason gets 6 Shillings a Day; fetch Whapsaws here, and Hatchets, and Augers, and Axes, and Spades, and Shovels, and Bibles, and Hammers, and Psalm Bukes, and Pots, and Seafaring Bukes, and fetch aw Sorts of Garden Seeds, Parsneps, Onions, and Carrots; and Potatoes grows here very big, red and white beth, fetch aw the Bukes here you can get, fetch a Spade, wee a Hoe made like a stubbing Ax, for ye may clear as muckle Grund for to plant Indian Corn, in ane Month, as will maintain Ten Folk for a Year. Dear Reverend Baptist Boyd, I hea been 120 Miles inn the Wolderness, and there I saw a Plain of Grund 120 Miles lang, and 15 Bred, and there never grew nor Tree upon it, and I hea see as gud Meadow grow upon it, as ever I see in Ereland. There is a great wheen of the Native Folks of this Country turn'd Christians, and will sing the Psalms bonily, and appear to be Religious, that gee Ministers plenty of Skins for his Steepend, and he gets Siller plenty for the Skins again; Deer Skins and Bear Skins: Ye may get Lan here for 10 L a Hundred Acres for ever, and Ten Years Time tell ye get the Money, before they wull ask ye for it; and it is within 40 Miles of this York upon a River Side, that this Lan lies, as that ye may carry aw the Guds in Boat to this York to sell, if ony of you comes here. It is a very strong Lan, rich Grund, plenty of aw Sorts of Fruits in it, and Swin plenty enough; There are Cay, and Stirks, and Horses that are aw wild in the Wolderness, that are aw yer ean when ye can grip them: desire my Fether and my Mether too, and my Three Sisters to come here, and ye may acquant them, there are Leds enugh here; and bid my Brether come, and I wull pay their Passage: Desire James Gibson to sell aw he has and come, and I weel help him too; for here aw that a Man warks for is his ane, there are ne ravenus Hunds to rive it fre us here, ne sick Word as Herbingers is kend here, but every yen enjoys his ane, there is ne yen to tak awa yer Corn, yer Potatoes, yer Lint or Eggs: na, na, blessed be his Name, ne yen gees Bans for his ane here.

I bless the Lord for my safe Journey here, I was Cook till the Ship aw the Voyage, we war Ten Weeks and Four Days on the See before we landed; this York is as big as twa of Armagh; I desire to be remembred to aw my Friends and Acquaintance, my Love to your sel Reverend Baptist Boyd, and aw yer femily; I do desire you to send this Letter to James Broon, of Drumern, and he kens my Brether James Gibson, and he weel gee him this Letter: It shall be my earnest Request yence mere, to beg of ye aw to come here, I did value the See ne mere then dry Lan: Let aw that comes here put in a gud Store of Otes Meel, and Butter, and Brandy, and Cheese, and Viniger, but above aw have a Writing under the Han of the Capden of the Ship ye come in; if I was now in Ereland, I wad ne stay there, yet I think to gang there as Factor for a Gentleman of this City of York, he is my Relation by my Father, he is Returney of the Law here. There is Servants comes here out of Ereland, and have serv'd their Time here, wha are now Justices of the Piece; I will come to Ereland gin the Lord spare me about Twa Years after this, and I wull bring Rum, and Staves for Barrals, and Firkins, and Tanners Bark for to sell, and mony other Things for this Gentlemen, and my sel, for I wull gang Super Cargo of the Ship, so that if none of ye come I wull bring ye aw wee my sel, by the Help of the Lord.

Now I have geen you a true Description of this York, luke the 8th Chapter of Deuteronomy, and what it saith of the Lan there, this is far better: Now this is the last of 6 Sheets I hea writt to you on this Heed, I hope that you Fether wull be stoor and come, and aw that I have named, fear ne the See, trust in God, and he wull bring ye safe to shore, gin ye plees him, now the Lord make ye so to do. Ne more fre me, but my Duty till my Fether and Mether, and Sisters and Brether, and yence mere my kind Love till yer sel, Reverend Mr. Baptist Boyd; if any yen sends me a Letter, direct till Mr. John Pemberton, Minister of the Gospel in New-York, send it we ony Body comin till ony of these Parts, and let it be given to the Post Hoose in America, and I will get it fre John Pemberton, and now my Love till ye aw.

James Murray

(1767 Version)

Address: For the Kingdom of Ereland in the North of Ereland, near Aghnacloy in the County of Tyrone, To Baptiste Boyd the Revarend Minister of the Gospel in the Parish of Aghnacloy. Let aw Persons that see this take Care to send it to the Revarend Baptiste Boyd, Minister of the Gospel in the Parish of Aghnacloy in the County of Tyrone living near Aughnacloy, wee Care.

Revarend Baptiste Boyd   March 18th 1767 New York

Read this Letter & look and tell aw the Poor folk of your place that God hath opened a Door for our deliverance, for here is nae scant of Breed here, & if your Son Samuel & John Boyd wad but come here they wad get mair money in ane Year for teeching a Latin School, nor your sell wad get for three Years preeching whar ye are. Ah Revd Baptist Boyd ther geed ane with me in the Ship, that new gets ane Hundred pounds ilka a year for the teeching & keeping a Latin School, and God kens, little was he skilled in Learning when I left ye, & new wad ye think it, I hea Twenty pounds a Year for being Clark till York Meeting House & I keep a School for wee weans –

Ah dear Sir there is braw liveing in this same toon for high Learned Men, the young folk in Ereland are aw but apack of Cowards, for I will tell you in short this is a bonny Country & aw things grows here that are I did see grow in Ereland, & we hae Cows and Sheep & Horses plenty here, & Goats & Deer & Raccoons & Beavers, & Fish & Fowls of aw sorts, Trades of aw sorts are gude here, a Wabster gets twelve pence a yard for a Tweel Hundred weaving, Eighteen pence for a Woolen Yard, a labourer gets four Shillings & Sax pence the Day, a Lassy gats four Shillings & sax pence the Week for spinin on the wee Lint wheele a Carpenter gets sax Shillings the Day, a Taylor gets twenty Shallings for making a Suit of Cleaths, a Wheelwright gets twenty Shallings for making lint Wheels apiece. Indian Corn a Man will git a heal Bushold of it for his Days work here, for Rye grows here, & Oats & Wheat & Winter Barley & Summer Barley and BuckWheat grows, na everything grow here – New I beg of ye aw to come here & bring our wee ye aw the Cleaths ye can of every Sort beath of Linen & Woolen & Guns & pooder & Shot & aw sorts of wars made of Iron & Steel and aw Tradesmen, let them bring their Tools wee them and Farmers their Plugh Irons, A Mason gits sax Shallings the Day, Fetch Wheep Saws here, & Hatchets & Augures & Axes, & Spades & Shovels & Bibles and Hamers & Salm Buckes fetch aw Sorts of Garden Seeds & Pots & Seafaring Buckes, & Parsnips & Onions, Kale & Karrots, fetch aw the Buckes here you can get, fetch a Spade & Hoe made like ane Stubbing Axe for here you may clare as muckle ground in ane Month as will maintain Tenfolk a heal Year.

Dear Revarend Doctor Baptiste Boyd, I hae been 120 Miles in the Wilderness and there I saw a plain 120 Miles long & 14 Bread & there never a Tree nor Bush on't & as gued Medow Ground as oney in Ereland, there are a great wheen of the native Folk of the Kintry turned Gued Christians & weel sing the Salms bonoly & appear Religious, & gee the Ministers plenty of Skins for his Steepings & he gits plenty of Siller for them again, Deer Skins to make Brecks of and Beaver Skins.

Revarend Doctor Baptist Boyd, ye may get Lan here for L 10 ane Hundred Acres for ever, & Ten Years forbearance till ye get the Money before they'll ask it fro you & it lies within 46 Miles fro this same York & upon a River Side it lies sae that ye can carry aw the Gueds in a Boat to this same York to sell if oney of you comes here it is a very strong Lan & very rich ground plenty of aw sorts of Fruit grows on it. Swine plenty enough – there are Kay & Stirks & Horses that are aw wild in the Wilderness & the are aw yer ane gin ye can grip them. Desire my Father & mither & my three Sisters till come here & I will pay aw their passages, desire James Gibson to sell aw he has & come here I will help him too, for here aw that a Man works for is his ane, there are nae ravenous Lans to rive it frae us here, nae sick a word as tythe or herbige is kenned here but ilk ane enjoys his ane, there is none till take away your Corn, yeer Keel, yere Potatoes, yere Lint, or yere Eggs, na, na, na, blessed be his Name, na ane gees bands for his ane Gueds here.

I bless the Lord for my safe Journey here, I was Cook till the Ship aw the Boyage [sic], we war ten Weeks & four days on the Sea afore we lawnded. – This same York is as big as twa of Armagh. I desire to be remembr'd to aw my Friends & Acquaintances my Loove to your Sell Reverand Baptiste Boyd & aw your gued Family, I do desire you till send this Letter till James Broon of Drumurn & he kens my Brither James Gibson & weel gae him this Letter, it shall be my earnist Request ance mair till beg of you aw till come here, I did value the Sea nae mare than the dry Lan, Let aw that come here put in a Sea Store of Oaten Meal & Butter & Brawndy & Cheese & Vinegar but above aw things have a writing under the Han of the Captain of the Ship, are ye come in, if I were in Ereland I would not stay there yet I thin[k] to gang there as a Factor to a Gentleman in this City, he is a Returney of the Law here, there are Servants here that came out of Ereland who are now Justices of the Peace, I wall come to Ereland, gin the Lord spare but twa Years after & will bring Rum & Staves for Barrels and Firkins for till sell & maney other things for this Gentleman & my sell for I will gang Super cargo of the Ship, sae that if nane of ye come afore I will bring ye aw wee me sell by the Help of the Lord. –

Now I have given you a true Description of this new York look untill the 8th Chapter of Deutoronomy & see what it saith of the Lan there, this is far better.

Now this is the last of sax Sheets of Paper I hae written to you upon this head I hope that your Father will be stoot & aw that I nam'd feer nae the Sea, trust in God & he will bring you safe to the Shore geen you please him Now the Lord make you aw so to do, nae mare frae me, but my Duty till my Father & Mither & my Sisters and Brithers & now ance mair to yere ane sell Reverand Doctor Baptiste Boyd, if oney ane write me a Letter direct to Mr. John Pemberton Minister of the Gospell in New York you may send it wee any body that is coming till these parts & it will come very safe and now my Love to aw Farewell

Jas Murray

[1] According to Susan Sullivan on the staff of the Presbyterian Historical Society in Philadelphia, there is no record of John Pemberton in the *Index of Presbyterian Ministers 1706-1871* by Willis Beecher or in the Society's own *Presbyterian Biographical Index*. Of course, Pemberton may possibly have been a clergyman in another denomination

[2] This volume was published by the Presbyterian Historical Society of Ireland, Belfast, in 1982. I am indebted to Dr Philip S Robinson of the Ulster Folk and Transport Museum for locating this information for me.

The common seal, numerous along the coast, is known as a silk 'selk'.

Mourne View

by Tom Porter
ORIGINALLY PUBLISHED IN ULLANS NUMMER 2, SPRING 1994

The isolation of the Mourne district of South Down is reflected in some of the dialect words used in the area. Many of these words are not known outside the district. Indeed, some are confined to small areas within the region. A recent survey of surnames shows that most names are of Scottish origin, and many of the dialect words appear to have been introduced by settlers during the seventeenth and eighteenth centuries. Words which appear to have Scandinavian origins may well have come by the Scottish route.

Sea and Shore
The common seal, numerous along the coast, is known as a *silk* 'selk', and a small island in the area bears that name. The small, inedible variety of crab is a *partin*, while the edible variety is a *crubin* (the word may be either singular or plural). The hook used to catch crabs is known as a *crubin cleek*. The inblown bladder wrack which farmers once collected for use as a fertiliser was locally known as *box*, and the coarse fronded variety, considered to be particularly good for growing turnips and marigolds, was *cam tails*. Anything cast up on the shore after a storm was *spoil*.

The species of whale which indicates the presence of a shoal of fish is known to the fishermen as the *hog* or *herring hog*, and the dog-fish, once considered as a kind of maritime vermin, is a *gabbock*. The coal-fish is locally known as a *blockan*, and the pollack as *lythe*. The young pollack is a *baahiv* and the grey gurnard is a *knowd*.

On the Land
When two or more farmers co-operate in a venture (eg *take* 'rent' land in conacre and share expense and labour), they are said to *work mean*. To *brerd* is to repair *ditches* with brushwood (*ditch* is used to refer to any type of field boundary with the exception of the wire fence). A tract of fenced mountain land is known as a *plan*, and a sheep-fold, normally enclosed by a stone ditch, is a *bucht*, as it is over much of Scotland.

A triangular-shaped field or tract of land is a *jib*, and short drills in an irregularly shaped field are *points*. Fields on low-lying land close to a river are often referred to as *holms*, and poor quality land is known as *beatens* or *grabbach*. The clamps in which potatoes were once stored were *pits*, and these were normally *happed* with *sprit* (sedge grass) and soil. Wrack or farmyard manure is *skailed* over the ground or in the *alleys* of drills, and a potato which has lain in the ground from a previous crop and has taken root is a *ground-keeper*. Potatoes which are considered too small for table use are *chats*. *Come in* and *hould off* as instructions to a horse indicate to turn left and right respectively. On the farm a length of rope was usually referred to as a *tether*, irrespective of its use. An armful of straw is a *wunnell*, a small stack is a *shig*, and a rectangular stack is a *havel*. The manually operated machine to separate chaff from grain was generally known as a *birler* from the spinning action of the fan. The fetter used to restrain animals, particularly sheep, is a *langle* (fore and rear leg) or *spancel* (fore legs), and the material used to mark sheep for identification purposes is *keel*.

Call Signs
Various terms are used to call domestic animals at feeding times: hens – *chooky*; turkeys – *pe*; pigs – *tory*; cows – *chey*; ducks – *wheety*; chicks – *birdie*; calves – *sook*.

A "CANNY WORD"

TO THE

DEMOCRATS O' THE WEST;

OR,

" What thé Deil wad ye be at ?"

A SONG.

To the Tune of—*" What the Pox wou'd ye be at ?"*

YE Democrats a'
 Wha mak a fraca',
Wha fcauld, an' wha gabble, an' prat,
 Gif ane o' ye kens well,
 Come here now a while,
An' tell's what the deil ye'd be at ?

 Hae ye na plenty
 O' what's haelfome and dainty ?
Wheat bread, meat an' milk, an' a' that;
 An' may, when you pleafe,
 Eat an' drirk at your eafe,
Then, what the deil wad ye be at ?

 Is there ony proud Laird
 To mak ye afeard,
To wh:m ye maun haud aff your hat ;
 Or ony great man,
 To rack-rent your land ?
Then what the deil wad ye be at ?

 Gif ane maks tranfgreffion
 On your gear or your perfon,
Ye ay can get mends in a crack;
 The Law's great ha' door
 Lets in rich an' poor,
Then, what the deil wad ye be at ?

David Bruce:
Ulster-Scot-American Poet

111

by Michael Montgomery
ORIGINALLY PUBLISHED IN ULLANS NUMMER 4, SPRING 1996

After a long period of neglect, poetry in Ulster Scots has in recent years begun to receive the attention it deserves. A watershed event was the publication in 1974 of John Hewitt's book *The Rhyming Weavers and Other Country Poets of Antrim and Down*. After a lifetime studying a school of working-class rural poets that flourished from the late-eighteenth to the mid-nineteenth century, Hewitt wrote this insightful account, to which he added selections from sixteen poets, all of whom wrote in Ulster Scots. More recently, the collected poetry of three early-nineteenth-century Weaver Poets (Hugh Porter, James Orr, and Samuel Thomson) has been published in separate volumes of the Folk Poets of Ulster series (Bangor: Pretani Press, 1992).

Although Hewitt tracked down hundreds of long-out-of-print verses written in Antrim and Down, he was apparently unaware that the writing of poetry in the Ulster-Scots language was rather more extensive. In fact, it was international, which is to say that it had spread to North America. It is well known that thousands of Ulster Scots emigrated to the newly opening continent in the 1700s, so it should be no surprise that some of them carried along a poetic muse. It will be instructive for us to examine and assess this matter in some detail. The poets Hewitt wrote about have yet to achieve more than a very modest reputation or recognition outside the north-east of Ireland. Hewitt identified connections between the Weavers and poets of Scotland, particularly Robert Burns, but this has led some literary critics to view (albeit erroneously) the Weavers as only a loose grouping of Burns imitators who happened to be from Ulster, where Burns was hardly less popular than on the Scottish mainland. Hewitt himself also viewed the school in fairly local terms.

The most notable of what may be called the 'Ulster-Scot-American' poets was David Bruce, whose 1801 collection, *Poems Chiefly in the Scottish Dialect, Originally Written under the Signature of the Scots-Irishman*, embodies the conviction that the Scots language was an entirely fit and effective medium for literary expression. Most of Bruce's poems appeared originally in the *Western Telegraphe and Washington Advertiser*, a weekly newspaper published in the western Pennsylvania town of Washington, near Pittsburgh, under the pseudonym 'The Scots-Irishman' (Bruce's name was revealed by the editor/printer of the collection, John Colerick). In the author's facility with the language and his choice of Scots over English for many of his verses we see a man who viewed Scots as appropriate for both serious and comic literary purposes. More important, Bruce's use of Scots implies that there must have been a considerable readership familiar with the language.

Who was David Bruce? Scholars have sketched a partial biography from comments in his poems. Born around 1760 and son to a farmer from Caithness, Scotland, he apparently spent his formative years in north County Londonderry, for he says of a compatriot,

> Ware na I sure yer' nae the same,
> I wad hae trow'd ye came frae hame,
> From Londonderry or Colrain.

Nothing is known of his education, though he may well have been self-taught. Nor is anything known of him from his arrival in Maryland in 1784 until he came to Burgettstown, Pennsylvania, in 1795. Establishing himself as a shopkeeper there, he became an active member of that community involved in political, real estate, and other affairs. It was state and national politics that most often prompted his poetry, which not only dealt with current events of the day, but often pilloried and bantered with public officials. The eastern part of the state had been settled by Europeans for well over a century, but Western Pennsylvania was frontier territory at the time. Bruce found the unfettered life there exhilarating, yet confounding. The new nation's experiment with democracy was taking uncertain, and sometimes alarming, turns, allowing men Bruce considered to be demagogues to have free rein and seeing many being misled by radical republicans intoxicated by the French Revolution. The time was a tumultuous one especially in the hills of Western Pennsylvania, where local rights had come to be sharply at odds with national laws in the so-called Whiskey Rebellion of 1794, which imposed a stiff tax on home-distilled liquor. The conflict, which was to smoulder for some time, chiefly pitted the common citizens of the area, the great majority of whom were of Ulster extraction and who supported the right to freely produce liquor for personal consumption, against the excise men of Philadelphia and Washington, and finally federal troops were ordered in by George Washington. Though he warmly praised the many qualities of good liquor, the elixir that he viewed as inspiring much of life's useful activity, Bruce accepted the tax and sided with the rule of law and the federal government on the issue. It is significant that, to express this allegiance, he was inspired to write his first poem in Scots, 'To Whiskey', four of the twenty-two stanzas of which follow:

I wat ye are a cunning chiel,
O' a' your tricks I ken fu' weel,
For aft ye hae gien me a heel,
  And thrown me down,
When I shook hands wi' heart so leel,
  Ye wily loun.

When fou o' thee on Irish grun',
At fairs I've aft' had muckle fun,
An' on my head wi' a guid rung,
  Gat mony a crack;
An' mony a braw chiel in my turn,
  Laid on his back.

   * * * * * * * *

But wou'd tak a leaf and mair
To tell o' a' your virtues rare;
At weddings, gossipping and fair,
  Baith great and sma'
Look unco dowff if ye'r na there,
  Great soul o' a'.

   * * * * * * * *

Then foul befa' the ungratefu' deil
That wou'd begrudge the pay right weel,
For a' the blessings that ye yiel.
  In sic a store;
I'd nae turn round upo' my heel
  For saxpence more.

Beneath the poem Bruce appended the following note, which gives some indication why he chose not to write in English:

> Poets (an airy race, who live on fame) are ever fond of seizing popular subjects; and what subject more popular at this time than Whiskey? The Author thought too, as the people, who are distinguished by the name of Scots-Irish, were the most numerous in the country, and were remarkable for their attachment to the subject of this Poem, to assume the language and appellation of a Scots-Irishman, would add to his celebrity.

Though not written in pure or deep Ulster Scots, there is much of the language in 'To Whiskey'. Some of the vocabulary is English, and some constructions (*your virtues rare*) reflect English poetic conventions. But the poem uses Scots on every line. Bruce employs conventional Scotticisms like *unco, muckle, guid*, and *ken*. The Scots forms *hae, mony, baith, sic*, and *deil* are used rather than English equivalents *have, many, both, such*, and *devil*. Final consonants are elided to produce *a'* 'all', *wi'* 'with', *fou* 'full', etc., all quite familiar to the ears of Lowland Scots and Ulster Scots.

Altogether, twenty-one other poems and songs in the volume are written in Scots, from 'The Author's Political Opinion' to 'A Canny Word to the Democrats of the West' to 'To Peter Porcupine'. This shows that Bruce did not employ the language in only a fanciful, experimental poetic effort extolling the 'water of life'. Interestingly, several of his fervent satires on Pennsylvania political officials were written in Scots, while he penned an elegy to Burns in English. Bruce wrote as an individual, not part of a group or school. We know he read Burns and Allan Ramsay, but there is no evidence that he was in touch with poets or even family members in Ulster or Scotland. We know of no followers or associates in Pennsylvania, but that he used Scots so freely and often suggests the existence of an audience that could appreciate his verse. It would be easy to imagine that there were others of his ilk in Western Pennsylvania and elsewhere in the American back country (the western or mountain portions of the Eastern states). Other than Bruce's own note cited above, we can surmise little other than that he felt entirely comfortable writing in Scots and must have believed it would secure an audience for himself.

There is little evidence that Bruce felt a strong ethnic affiliation. His adopted pseudonym implies that he welcomed being identified as a Scot from Ireland, but his writing dealt with American topics and almost never touched on national or ethnic groups in the new nation. He stated that the Scots and Irish often formed the backbone of British armies, yet he was more adamant against the French than the British cause in the 1790s. He feared the influence of French revolutionary ideas in the United States, but made no reference, at least in his poetry, to their role in Ireland, which contributed to the Irish rebellion of 1798.

Bruce lived nearly thirty years beyond the publication of his one volume of poems. He maintained his shopkeeping until his death in 1830 and in later years became an elder of his community of Burgettstown, as many sought him for advice. Much earlier in his career he had written 'An Advice to Old Bachelors' (in English) repudiating the blessed estate of matrimony. He followed this counsel well and was buried beneath a simple stone in the United Presbyterian Cemetery in Burgettstown.

Bruce must have spoken Ulster Scots regularly, which is itself hardly surprising. Emigrants take their language and other cultural luggage with them. But that he wrote in Ulster Scots is far more significant. It indicates that Ulster Scots was for a time an international language, that it could, at least to a slight degree, compete with English abroad, and that a fair number of people must have been literate in Scots, at least in some places. Bruce's writing and that of others indicates that the Western Pennsylvania frontier was a very diverse place. In addition to Amerindian languages, French, German, and other European tongues, there were at least four related varieties from the British Isles: Lowland Scots, Ulster Scots, British English, and Irish English. And then there was the newly developing American English, to which all four contributed. But that is a subject for another occasion.

The author is grateful to the G Ross Roy Collection of Burns, Burnsiana, and Scottish Poetry at the University of South Carolina for making available a copy of David Bruce's volume of poetry for consultation.

Excerpts from the Poetry of David Bruce:

A 'CANNY WORD' to the Democrats of the West;
or, 'What the Deil wad ye be at?'
A SONG

> Ye Democrats a'
> Wha mak a fraca',
> Wha scauld, an' wha gabble, an' prat,
> Gif ane o' ye kens well,
> Come here now a while,
> An' tell's what the deil ye'd be at?

> Hae ye na plenty
> O' what's haelsome and dainty?
> Wheat bread, meat an' mil, an' a' that;
> An' may, when you please,
> Eat an' drink at your ease,
> Then, what the deil wad ye be at?

> Is there ony proud Laird
> To mak ye afeard,
> To whom ye maun haud off your hat;
> Or ony great man,
> To rack-rent your land?
> Then what the deil wad ye be at?

To My Musie

Ye paukie, wanton, hum'rous witch!
Had'n't been for ye, I might been rich
For Fortune's nae sic a blind bitch,
        As people say;
She aft will gie a lucky hitch,
        When ane's i' th' way.

She's just like a' the rest o' your sort,
Gif ye wou'd hae her, ye maun court,
An' he wha maks the best push for't,
    Wi' bauld advance--
It is nae aft that he comes short
    O' a good chance.

But this to ye does nae alude;
For should ane o' the forward crowd
Come to court ye, pert, brazen-brow'd--
    Lord! how you'd gloom!
You're nae light taupie, wha'd be woo'd
    By ony loun.

Soon Fun:
A Quiz on Ulster-Scots

by Elspeth Barnes
ORIGINALLY PUBLISHED IN ULLANS NUMMER 5, SIMMER 1997

Match the words in the first column to the words in the second column. All the words look 'English', but use Ulster-Scots meanings and sounds to pair them off. For example, *bait* would be paired with *lick* because both mean 'to beat'.

1	Answer	A	Bed		1	-	M	(both words mean 'to suit')
2	Bad	B	Croon		2	-	L	(both words mean 'sick')
3	Brave	C	Fox		3	-	E	(*brave lock* means 'good number')
4	Breed	D	Grew		4	-	J	(both words mean 'bread')
5	Clock	E	Lock		5	-	O	(both words mean 'to brood' [of a hen])
6	Collie	F	Mane		6	-	C	(*collie fox* means 'to mislead, trick')
7	Dug	G	Moose		7	-	D	(both words mean 'dog')
8	Gavel	H	Pickle		8	-	T	(*gavel windy* means 'gable window')
9	Greet	I	Pie		9	-	K	(both words mean 'to cry')
10	Heed	J	Piece		10	-	B	(both words mean 'head')
11	Howl	K	Roar		11	-	P	(*howl study* means 'hold steady, stand still')
12	Merry	L	Seek		12	-	S	(both words mean 'to wed')
13	Near	M	Set		13	-	F	(both words mean 'mean')
14	Poor	N	Sin		14	-	Q	(both words mean 'to pour')
15	Settle	O	Sit		15	-	A	('settle-bed')
16	Screw	P	Study		16	-	G	('shrew mouse')
17	Simmer	Q	Tim		17	-	N	('summer sun')
18	Square	R	Toy		18	-	I	(both words mean 'pay')
19	Taste	S	Wad		19	-	H	(both words mean 'some')
20	Tig	T	Windy		20	-	R	(*tig-toy* means 'tease')

Ulster-Scots landmark stone (Dunloy, County Antrim)

What is Ulster Scots?

by Michael Montgomery
ORIGINALLY PUBLISHED IN ULLANS NUMMER 8, HAIRST 2001

I reland lies on the periphery of Europe, but it has long been a cross-roads, as people from many directions – Britain, Scandinavia, Iberia, and elsewhere – have come to its shores to settle. In the process of doing so they have brought different languages with them. A millennium ago or so speakers of Germanic (Old English, Old Norse) and Romance (Norman French) tongues arrived to join (and often assimilate to) a Celtic-speaking population. The results of these migrations can be seen today on Ireland's linguistic landscape, especially in its place names.

Historical accounts usually sketch a succession of languages competing with and supplanting one another in Ireland. English was a relative late-comer, arriving with Anglo-Normans in the twelfth century. The fortunes of Irish Gaelic and English since Elizabethan times have affected life on the island in innumerable and profound ways, so it is not surprising that relations between these languages have preoccupied language historians and given rise to the view that the island's language situation has in recent centuries been a dichotomous one.

However, the Irish vs. English picture of language relations obscures what has differentiated Ulster from the rest of Ireland. For example, a Scottish type of Gaelic came (some might prefer to say 'returned') to north-east Ulster in the fourteenth century from the Western Isles and Highlands of Scotland. Dwarfing these Gaelic speakers in number, however, were Scots mainly from the west-central and southwestern Lowlands coming in the seventeenth century. With relatively few exceptions, these settlers arrived speaking not Gaelic or English, but the Germanic tongue Scots, and they extended the territory of this language to much of Ulster. In the migration of languages and in countless other comings and goings, the narrowness of the north channel of the Irish Sea (scarcely a dozen miles from Fair Head to the Mull of Kintyre) made, according to one historian, the 'connexion between West Scotland and North-east Ireland ... a constant factor in history'.[1] This proximity was pivotal in giving Ulster its own linguistic diversity. In other words, what more than anything else differentiates the linguistic landscape of Ulster from the rest of Ireland today is the presence of the Scots language's Ulster form, Ulster Scots.

The migration of languages and their ensuing relations in Ulster might seem to be of interest to scholars alone, and until the early 1990s this was the case. Until a decade ago information on Ulster Scots could be found in only a few scholarly tomes and academic journals, and these were usually published abroad. Today a significant proportion of Northern Ireland's population recognizes the term 'Ulster Scots' and its newer alternative 'Ullans' amid increased discussion of cultural and linguistic diversity in Northern Ireland. A revival of Ulster Scots is in progress. Two watershed events have been the founding of the Ulster-Scots Language Society and its magazine *Ullans* in 1992 and establishment of the Ulster-Scots Agency in 1999 as part of the new cross-border language body created under the Good Friday Agreement. One of the agency's most recent accomplishments is the launching of the Institute of Ulster-Scots Studies at the Magee College site of the University of Ulster in January 2001.

Lively public discussion of language issues has followed the increasing visibility given Ulster Scots. Information on the language is now more widely available and the serious study of Ulster-Scots history, culture, and literature is expanding. However, the public discussion in Northern Ireland has often been animated and sometimes derisive, and very often predictable and repetitious, with people often relying on personal experience, preconceptions, and political orientation rather than serious or open-minded consideration. Some assert that Ulster Scots is a 'recent invention', others that it has an 'ancient heritage'. More and more believe that it deserves government recognition and support. The Good Friday Agreement of April 1998 is the first official document to mention Ulster Scots, stating in part that:

> all participants recognize the importance of respect,
> understanding and tolerance in relation to linguistic diversity,
> including in Northern Ireland, the Irish language, Ulster Scots
> and the languages of the various ethnic communities, all of
> which are part of the cultural wealth of the island of Ireland.

This statement indicates that formal recognition of Ulster Scots is expected to play a role in the continuing Northern Ireland peace process.

I will not consider the question here of the status of Ulster Scots, ie whether it is a 'language or a dialect', at least not directly. Linguists do not agree on how best to define these terms. They do agree that this distinction is simplistic and usually artificial and that it cannot be used meaningfully to classify a large number of the world's thousands of tongues. They agree that among other traits a language has a historic speech community, its own grammatical rules, and stylistic differences. Further, they agree that in a profound way it is speakers themselves to whom the right belongs to designate the speech of their historic community to be a 'language' or a 'dialect'. This principle of self-definition is of crucial importance. Linguists are willing to see a separate history as one element that makes a form of speech worthy of the designation 'language'. They are less inclined to use political, demographic, or cultural factors than non-linguists are in assessing a variety's status and identity. However, they do agree that the views of native speakers should be taken into account in assessing status, and these views may be decisive.

There are five points about which scholars have formed a consensus regarding Ulster Scots.

First, scholars generally consider Ulster Scots to be a regional variety of Scots. The latter is a close sibling to English and is the historic language of Lowland Scotland. Any assessment of the status of Ulster Scots rests on an assessment of Lowland Scots. Having a common source with English in the Anglo-Saxon of a thousand years ago, Scots in some respects has remained closer to its roots than has British English. In the fifteenth and sixteenth centuries it became an all-purpose, national language, used as the medium for education, literature, law, and the royal court in Scotland.

Toward the end of the 1500s the written form of Scots began to erode on the advance of English, and it slowly disappeared except for certain limited, especially poetic, uses. Its spoken forms persisted, and today vernacular Scots remains distinct from English in countless ways in its pronunciation, vocabulary, and grammar. Because it has no role in public or institutional life, however, its status as a language is less clear-cut than in centuries past.

Beyond its history and a distinguished tradition of literature, other factors support the status of Scots as a language. It has many dialects of its own, including several used in local literature today in both Scotland and Ulster. Its long and vigorous tradition of dictionaries surpasses that of many continental languages, of special note being the 12-volume *Dictionary of the Older Scottish Tongue* and the 10-volume *Scottish National Dictionary*. Further, Scots is a subject of study in its own right at Edinburgh and Glasgow Universities.

Despite its loss of prestige in relation to English, Scots has long been considered inseparable from Scottish cultural life and the identity of Scotland as a nation. According to Professor A J Aitken:

> Nonetheless, despite stigmatization in school, neglect by
> officialdom, and marginalization by the media, people of all
> backgrounds since the 16 c[entury] insisted in regarding the guid
> Scots tongue as their national language, and it continues to play
> an important part in people's awareness of their national identity.

This view is held by a cross-section of Scotland's population today, from literati to educators on all levels to the general populace, including many who do not speak Scots, and it may now be on the increase, given growing national consciousness and the recent reinstitution of the Scottish Parliament after nearly 300 years.

Scots is most appropriately seen today as a regional language that under the pressure of English has lost many of its functions, particularly for writing. It is now far from a fully-fledged language like English, French, or German, but this hardly denies it the status of language on other grounds.

Family letters and legal documents from Scottish settlers in Ulster in the seventeenth century reveal that Scots was their primary language. Through plantation schemes and less formal migrations, tens of thousands of Lowland Scots arrived in Ulster in the first third of that century, forming a rural heartland that further movement from Scotland and internal migration expanded in succeeding decades. As many as 100,000 Lowlanders had come to Ulster by 1700, in the course of which Ulster Scots became the only recognizable variety of Scots outwith the mainland of Scotland. English became the language of urban life, education, commerce, government, social institutions, and writing in Ulster. Though it absorbed elements from Ulster Scots and Irish Gaelic, it relegated both of them to the countryside and the home. There Ulster Scots has remained a medium of daily life in parts of four counties (Down, Antrim, Londonderry, and Donegal) and has now had a stable community of speakers for four hundred years. According to James Milroy, a linguist originally from Scotland, 'In the Scots areas there are a great many rural speakers who speak a dialect of Scots rather than English: in its strongest forms it is almost indistinguishable from the Scots dialects of West and Central Scotland. The Scots character of these Ulster dialects is most salient in the pronunciation of common lexical items'.[2] In short, Ulster Scots is unmistakably Scots.

A second point of consensus is that Ulster Scots today is foremost a spoken variety of language. Its character, distinctiveness, and vitality lie in the speech of the rural areas settled by Scots in the seventeenth century, especially after the Ulster Plantation in 1610. Though its written form that was brought from Scotland disappeared quickly, research on church records, emigrant letters, and other documents provides indirect evidence that spoken Ulster Scots has thrived continuously on the ground over the past four centuries. More direct evidence is that Ulster Scots has from time to time found a voice in a literature of its own that, though limited in scope and genre, has been grounded in speech. Collectively this literature shows that Ulster Scots has remained available, sometimes preferable, for written purposes.

Two principal periods of literary expression can be identified. One lasted from the 1780s through the mid-1850s and involved the 'Weaver' poets, a school of popular versifiers who wove linen by trade. Many of them assumed the stance of community spokesmen and were given nicknames signifying this. James Orr (1770-1816), perhaps the most notable of them, was called the 'Bard of Ballycarry'. This poetic movement drew from local themes and was by no means a mere imitation or derivation from Robert Burns' work. A definitive account, *The Rhyming Weavers*, was authored by John Hewitt in 1974.

Another stage of Ulster-Scots literature began in the 1850s and extended well past 1900. It consisted of popular sketches, commentaries, and stories that appeared in local newspapers in Antrim and Down (an example was the work of W G Lyttle, who wrote for the *Newtownards Chronicle* in the 1880s and 1890s). These items were typically written in a folksy first-person style and addressed a range of social and political topics and issues. This literature also saw itself as a voice of the people and was strikingly paralleled in Scottish newspapers of the same period. Ulster-Scots literature is important for what it reveals of everyday life and society of former times and the creative skills of individual writers, but its greater significance lies in its implication that spoken Ulster Scots has had a distinctive character and continuous existence for centuries.

A third point of consensus is that Ulster Scots has both regional and social dimensions. Forty years ago Robert Gregg mapped its geographical boundaries. That Ulster Scots is a regional folk variety long confined to the countryside is indicated by its extensive vocabulary for rural and domestic life and by the fact that Catholics speak it as well as Protestants in the same districts. According to James Fenton, author of *The Hamely Tongue: A Personal Record of Ulster-Scots in County Antrim*, 'its use rarely depends on the social or material status of speakers, and never at all on their political or religious convictions'.[3] Apparently all speakers of Ulster Scots also command one or more varieties of English. Because it lacks prestige in comparison with English, however, Ulster Scots even within its core region gives way today in certain situations (especially in the presence of outsiders or those having social authority), in certain locales (especially towns), for certain subject matter, and for speakers having or seeking greater education or social position.

I do not wish to imply that the boundary between Ulster Scots and English is a strict one. In many respects it is not. Though the extreme forms of English and Ulster Scots are quite distinct, the two languages form a structural, stylistic, and geographical continuum with many intermediate varieties. At one end is unmonitored rural Ulster

Scots as used in its core territory and exhibiting distinctive Scots features such as *toon* 'town' and *dinnae* 'do not', fully comprehensible only to native speakers. At the other extreme is what is in this part of the world called 'Standard English'.

Because of this continuum Ulster Scots has an utterly different relation to English than does Irish Gaelic, but one similar to that often found in continental Europe between historically related language varieties like Low German and High German (the latter being the modern standard variety). In northern Germany, vernacular Low German is used in the home, High German in the school, and mixed varieties in social interaction. Within the Ulster-Scots speech community most speakers command two or three varieties along the English/Ulster-Scots scale, so they can in some sense be described as bilingual. They have acquired through education, employment or contact one or more varieties of English, which they use with non-speakers of Ulster Scots. Over the years many natives of Northern Ireland, particularly in Belfast, have remarked to me that they don't believe Ulster Scots exists (even though Gregg's Ulster-Scots territory comes within a few miles of the city) because they have never heard it. This means simply that they are not themselves speakers of Ulster Scots and that native speakers recognize this and use only English when speaking with them.

A fourth point of agreement is that, as a result of continuing pressure from English and mainstream culture, Ulster Scots is now stigmatized. Until quite recently it had no status or recognition outside its home communities in the countryside except, to a limited extent, in academia. Mistakenly labeled 'poor English', it has long been denigrated and suppressed by the educational system and scorned in polite society, the object of censure and social prejudice. In the popular mind, speaking Ulster Scots usually came to represent inferior social class and a lack of education. Without positive associations in the culture at large, Ulster Scots became, not surprisingly, covert. It is used only with other native speakers, as a result of which there are almost no recordings of it. Even in remote rural districts the typical visitor may hear many linguistic features of Scottish ancestry in the local speech, but never Ulster Scots as a variety of language *per se*.

What then accounts for the continuing vitality of Ulster Scots? Why has it survived at all? For generations English has been the language of wider society, economic mobility, and power, so the survival of Ulster Scots must be due to the strength and cohesiveness of its culture and the solidarity of its speakers and their speech communities.

A final point is that Ulster Scots is declining, even within its limited domain. This has very often been overstated (eg it was predicted over a century ago to occur in another generation or two), but the precise nature of this 'decline' deserves, along with many other topics, careful investigation by scholars. There can be no doubt that at present Ulster Scots is endangered. Language choice and survival is ultimately democratic, often brutally so. People decide for themselves whether to keep their language of nurture or replace it. If Ulster Scots is to survive, its native speakers must consciously choose to maintain it. All the language planning, official support, required study, and inducements in the world cannot ensure that a language not considered serviceable by a native-speaking community will endure, much less flourish. Irish is a prime example of this in modern Europe.

In sum, Ulster Scots is recognized by scholars as a historic spoken variety of Scots used in rural Ulster for four hundred years, a mode of expression maintained in the home and community but having had little public use and no institutional life. Within its territory it varies geographically and socially, and it has a non-discrete relationship with English. Because of great pressure from English, it now has low prestige and is on the decline. Ulster Scots has many limitations, most notably its lack of modern vocabulary, since it is tied to an eroding folk culture, and in real-world terms it is and will remain inferior to English in many ways. However, it is unreasonable to say that either Ulster Scots or Lowland Scots is a 'dialect of English' simply because it is not a 'fully fledged language'.

A different way of looking at languages is that adopted by the European Bureau for Lesser-Used Languages (EBLUL), an agency of the Council of Europe that has fostered public education and awareness of what it calls 'regional' and 'minority' languages, terms that until recently would have been oxymorons for many Europeans. Under the European Charter for Regional and Minority Languages approved in 1992, the Council of Europe agreed that ' ... the protection of the historical regional or minority languages of Europe, some of which are in danger of eventual extinction, contributes to the maintenance and development of Europe's cultural wealth and traditions'. EBLUL's approach is applicable to western European varieties of language like Ulster Scots that have a close genetic relationship to a dominant language of power, literacy, and nationhood.

According to the European charter, a minority language is one 'traditionally used within the territory of a State by nationals of that State who form a group numerically smaller than the rest of the State's population and different from the official languages of that State'. The genetic relation of a minority language is either distant, if it exists at all, to an official or national language (eg Irish and English in Northern Ireland) or it is quite close, of the same branch of the family (eg English and Scots). The European

Charter extends the category of minority language from the first type, which has long been recognised, to the second, because the two types of languages have similar real-world dimensions. They stand in the same political and social relation to a modern national language. However, lacking a clear identity, languages of the second type (forty of which have now been recognized by EBLUL) have for centuries been considered dialects, sometimes non-entities. These include Occitan in France, Valencian in Spain, and Friulian in Italy.

Within a European context, Ulster Scots is a rather typical regional language. Its history dates to the Early Modern period, it has close kinship with the official language of the nation (English), but it has been marginalized in recent centuries. The work of EBLUL highlights the ideology of modern western cultures when it comes to language status. One can hardly overestimate how far educational systems have used the idea of the centralized nation state to deny the value and sometimes the existence of regional cultures. In western Europe spoken varieties are inevitably belittled because of their lack of a written tradition or a standard spelling system.

When written, a full account of Ulster Scots will profoundly affect our understanding of the linguistic history of Ireland. It will throw into sharp relief the necessity of seeing the language situation in Ulster over the past four centuries as pluralistic and trilingual, involving continuing contact between English, Scots, and Irish Gaelic and the influence of each upon the others. Along with this will come a fuller appreciation of the complexity of language variation in the British Isles in the modern era.

We must surely agree with the Good Friday Agreement that Ulster Scots deserves recognition. Though declining like many regional languages, it is very far from disappearing and in a few short years has made major strides. In the larger community it is of value because of the community and the tradition it represents. If it is to play a role in the building of mutual understanding in Ireland, it must be seen within its proper context as representing one of three historic language traditions in Ulster.

NOTES:
[1] G M Trevelyan, *A Shortened History of England* (Baltimore, 1959), 60
[2] J Milroy, *Regional Accents of English: Belfast* (Belfast, 1981), 23
[3] J Fenton, *Platform*, January 1995

For further reading, consult the following:
Montgomery, Michael. 1999. 'The Position of Ulster Scots' *Ulster Folklife* 45. 85 – 104
Montgomery, Michael, and Robert Gregg. 'The Scots Language in Ulster' *The History of Scots*, ed. by Charles Jones, 569 – 622. Edinburgh: Edinburgh University Press

SAMPLE HISTORICAL TEXTS OF ULSTER SCOTS

1 I Sir Robert McClellane of Bomby knight be thir presentis does
   faithfullie promeiss to my gud freynd David Cunynghame of Heurt
   his airis and assignayis to set to thame ane sufficient Laice of twell scoir
   aikeris of land that I haif of the Happerdaschers portion of Londary
   and that for the space of one and fiftie yeirs lyand within the Countie
   of Culraine in ony pairt of the said Happerdaschers proportioun now
   perteyning to me exceptand and reservand the stone hous and mannis ...
   (Robert McClelland of Bomby Legal Documents,
   Public Record Office of Northern Ireland, 1614).

2 W Houstoun to [name missing], April 25th, 1626, Ballemeanaghe:
   'Worschipfull, my deuty unto your self rememberit and not forgetting
   my deuty and service to my Lord Clanneboyes. Theis ar to put yow in
   remembrance and also to intreate yow to do me the favour that ye
   wilbe in Craigfergus on Monday nixt, being May day, that I may haif
   your contenance thair at the tendur of Abrey Loo his money, as also
   for my meitting with Jhone McCulloch, becaus ye ar the man chosin
   for me as it fallis by our submissioun. Sunday nixt was the day of our
   meitting, bot I think we must put it off till Tuesday next. This hoiping ye
   will perform as I schalbe ever reddy to yow in the lyik of anything ellis
   that lyes in my power, and sua remaines, your faithfull freind, V. Houstoun.
   ('Historical Manuscripts Commission 1909: 123 – 24)

3 Nae mair shall I gang, while in this side o' time ...
   Nae mair, while ilk mouth's clos'd, an' fast the door bar'd,
   Initiate the novice, baith curious and scaur'd;
   Nae mair join wi' scores in the grand chorus saft,
   Nor fandly toast 'Airlan' – and peace to the craft';
   I aye cud been wi' ye, but now I maun stay
   Confin'd in my lang hame – the cauld house o' clay.
   (James Orr, c.1790)

4   Newtownards Chronicle, 18th November 1882

AN ECHT-DAYS RETROSPECK O CUMMER DOINS
To the editur o the 'Newtoun Chronickel'

SUR – You wull nae doot wunner at my lang silonse, but the
awfu things that hae hapened ye ken gies me a terble time o
truble, gest to think that ony thief can gang intil yer back
yeard and steel pig troughs, and make three-legged pots rin
awa wi hachets is enuff to mack yen's hair stan on thar heed;
and day a this, mind ye, an get off scot frae. It ocurs to my
mind that the star wi the lang tale has sumthin to day wi
these miricals, but mebbe the aturney wha sayed sich quare
things ti the fella that the pot and ither things rin awa frae
hes som nollege o astronmy, and caused the lang tailed comit
to dezzel the eyes o folk a could name, wha think it no crime
to day the like …

(W G Lyttle, 1882).

Sir Robert McClelland of Bombie, Plantation Land Agent

ORIGINALLY PUBLISHED IN ULLANS NUMMER 4, SPRING 1996

S ir Robert McClelland was a distinguished Scottish laird from Kircudbrightshire who became the agent for the Haberdashers and Clothworkers Company in north Derry in the early days of King James' Plantation of Ulster. Documents written by himself or his Scottish aides are very different from those written at the same time by English planters. In the document below, typical Scots spellings and orthographic forms (such as *quh-* for *wh-*) abound.

Sir Robert McClelland (Agent for Clothworkers Company)

'Letter of Promise of a Lease of Haberdashers Lands in County Londonderry to David Cunningham', October 21, 1614

I Sir Robert McClellane of Bomby knight be[1] thir[2] presentis dois[3] faithfullie promeiss to my gud freynd David Cunynghame of Heurt his airis[4] and assignayis to set to thame ane[5] sufficient Laice of twell[6] scoir aikeris[7] of land that I haif of the Happerdaschers[8] portioun of Londary and that for the space of one and fiftie yeirs lyand[9] within the Countie of Culraine[10] in any pairt of the said Happerdaschers proportioun now pertenying to me exceptand and reservand the stone hous and mannis his toun village and mylne[11] and toun lands lyand thairto that the said Sir Robert pleiss chois best quhilk[12] twell scoir akeris of land sall[13] ly all and togidder[14] guid arrabill and pastuirabill Payand thairfoir yeirlie for ilk[15] aiker the sowme of tuell penis sterling money and that for all uther rent and dewtie can be askit[16] be me the said Sir Robert or his foirsaids and gif[17] thair be not peit and turff within the said xij [ie xii] scoir aiker of land I the said Sir Robert promissis that David Cuningham and his foirsaids shall haif sufficient peit and turff yeirlie in the nixt adjacent[18] moss thairto with ane sufficient way for carrying thame to thair houssis As also gif it salhappin me the said Sir Robert and my foirsaids[19] to obtene ane Laice of the teithis of these Landis the said Sir Robert and my foirsaids promissis faithfullie that the said David his foirsaids shall haife ane sufficient richt[20] thairoff of the cheapest rent that only uther my friends sall haiff possessours of these landis As also I the said Sir Robert binds me and my foirsaids for the guidwill and favour I beir to the said David Cunynghame to gif hym and his foirsaids ane hundreth[21] aikers of the said twell scoir aikers frie in a coppyhold gif he pieis to accept thairof payand thairfor yeirlie for ilk aiker of the said hundreth a grote[22] sterling money and sall gif hym and thame a sufficient richt thairoff. And further I the said David obleis me and my foirsaidis to cum to the said Sir Robertis mylnnes nixt adjacent thairto and pey the multouris[23] thairto as utheris his freyndis and coppyholderis dois and to keip his courtis and giff obedience thairto as becummis being haldin within the said proportioun and farther I obleys me to build ane sufficient and strang[24] hous of the Ingliss[25] forme or ellis with stone gif I can haif thame esily As also I bind me and my foirsaidis to serve the said Sir Robert and his foirsaids in all his and thair lesum effair quhen I and my foirsaidis guidlie may without harme to our selffis. In Witnes heiroff I haiff signet seillit and subscrywit this samin with my hand at Newtoun the twentie ane day of October Befoir Mr William and John Schawis and William and Thomas MccLellans my servandis[26].

Bombye (L.S.)

    William Schau.
    Jhone Schaw, witnes.
    Thomas Mccelland, witnes.

[1] by
[2] these
[3] does, do
[4] heirs
[5] one, an, a
[6] twelve
[7] acres (note the *-is* plural ending on this and other nouns)
[8] Haberdashers
[9] lying (note the *-and* ending on this and other present participles)
[10] County Londonderry was known as County Coleraine before the plantation.
[11] mill
[12] which
[13] shall
[14] together
[15] each
[16] asked (note the *-it* ending on this and other past-tense forms of regular verbs)
[17] if
[18] peat bog
[19] representatives
[20] right
[21] hundred
[22] groat (13s 4d)
[23] multure (the proportion of meal ground at the mill provided to the miller)
[24] strong
[25] English
[26] servants

His holl canone was drownit with a grit pairt of his army.

The Oul Leid:
John Hamilton of Bangor

ORIGINALLY PUBLISHED IN ULLANS NUMMER 5, SIMMER 1997

The following example of old Ulster-Scots writing is a letter written in 1627 by John Hamilton of Bangor. It was sent from the wars in Germany to Archibald Edmonstone of Ballycarry. John Hamilton (Jhone Hammyltone) was one of four sons of William Hamilton of Bangor, whose own father had been a minister in Dunlop, Ayrshire. William and each of his four sons were styled of 'Newcastle' alias 'Bangor'. In fact, County Down had numerous places called 'Newcastle' from time to time, including a 'Newcastle in the Airds' near Cloghey in the Ards Peninsula.

All four of William Hamilton's sons became army captains. James, the first son, was killed in 1646 at the Battle of Benburb, County Tyrone, fighting for the Scots Covenanters under General Munro. John, the second son, became a captain along with Hans and William, the third and fourth sons. Archibald Edmonstone of Red Hall, Ballycarry, was the Laird of Duntreath. The Edmonstones had originally come from Ayrshire to Greyabbey in County Down with the Montgomerys, but had moved to Antrim shortly after.

In the letter, mention is made by James Hamilton of one of his 'lieutenants' in Germany with him. This was James Wachope from the Haw ('Hall') at Haw Hill, Kilmore, County Down, and another of his 'sogers' was 'Wilzame Boyd, sone to Dawid Boyd in the Airdis'. This David Boyd was the same Colonel David Boyd who accompanied Sir Hugh Montgomery in his first plantation of the Ards in 1605. In 1609 Colonel David Boyd was granted the lands of Ballymacarrett from Montgomery, to add to the extensive lands throughout north Down and the Ards which he received in 1607. The 1607 grant of lands to David Boyd had several townlands around Greyabbey reserved for Archibald Edmonstone. Indeed, Edmonstone lived at Greyabbey for about seven years before moving to the lands at Ballycarry and the castle of Red Hall (Read Haw), which he acquired in 1609. David Boyd established his main dwelling at Ballycastle (formerly Castleton), near Mountstewart, in the Ards Peninsula.

Note that the mixed Scots-English nature of this letter becomes more Scots in the middle when the writer gets into his stride.

Jhone Hammyltone to Archibald Edmonstone
(Tidings of the progress of the war in Germany)

1627, December 25th

Right honourable, Having this occasione of your servant I ame bauld to remember my deuty to yours wourthie mother, to yours saielfe and laday, with all the rest of that honorabill famely. Pleis yow, the overthrew gifing to the Deuik is marvelouse grit. Thaire is ane grit army preparing in Ingland quhairto yit not knawing. For this effeck thair is ane Parliament be in Scotland schortlie. My lieutennant, James Wachope, with many uthers offisars ar laitlie arrivit frome Germany to lewie sogers for the use of the King of Denmarck. He hes gifing Count Tily ane marvelousie grit defaiet. Tylie is army biing passit ower the river of Allfe [Alster] the King of Denmark causit in the nicht for a lontyme labour and wourk till he cuttit the rivar and maied it rin within Tyly is army quhar thaire his holl canone was drownit with a grit pairt of his army. The rest flying could not fall bot one the army of the King quhar they all for the most pairt war put to the suourd. Thus we have hard frome Dublein, sence frome Ingland, [and] now Jamis Wachope, as we ar informit, reportis the same. He hes bein this fourtnicht past at Port Patrick and cane nocht wune over, bot thaire come ane bot frome Loche Rying quharin thaire was ane mane boithe spak him saielfe and did sie Jamis Wachope. Quhat neuis I sall have you sall heir frome me as occasionis fallis out. I ame affrayid I sall nocht returne home now till Mairche, that I may carry with me all my pipill. Pleas yow, gud Sir, thaire is niver ane soger of myne athar went avay from any leutennant or deid sence thair pairteur bot ane Wilzame Boyd, sone to Dawid Boyd in the Airdis. I heir he was ane insolent youthe; he deiit of ane flux. The namis of thous ar killit and prisoners I have sent yow, bot favour me soe muche that I may have it agane quhen yow sall send any over to thir pairtis. I ame and all yours humbell trew servant, J HAMMYLTONE.

Advertising Poster for Scotch Tweeds - Letterkenny, Co. Donegal

'Scotch Poems' from East Donegal in 1753

Commentary by Ronnie R Adams
ORIGINALLY PUBLISHED IN ULLANS NUMMER 1, SPRING 1993

In the year 1753 a stout volume entitled *The Ulster Miscellany* was printed in Belfast. As the title suggests, this consisted of a number of items, including 'A voyage to O'Brazeel, a sub-marine Island, lying west off the coast of Ireland', but in many ways the most interesting section is a collection of verses entitled 'Scotch poems'. These nine poems were all written in the Laggan area of east Donegal. The authors were anonymous, and their collection of Ulster-Scots verse represents the first substantial one in print in that language, published before Robert Burns was born. As a native of that area of Donegal myself, this is a matter of some pride. The following verses illustrate the exasperation of a Laggan farmer at the tithe-gathering efforts of the local Established Church clergyman.

TIT for TAT; or the Rater rated.
A new song, in Way of Dialogue, between a
Laggen farmer and his Wife.

HE   Ye're welcome hame, my Marg'y,
       Frae the grim craving clergy;
       How deeply did they charge ye,
          Wi' fair oppressive tythe?
       While some are chous'd, and cheated;
       Some rattled are, and rated;
       Ye hae been better treated,
          I trow, ye luick sae blythe.

SHE   I hae been wi' the rector;
       His wife did scould and hector;
       Instead o' a guid lecture -
          Quo' she, 'Ye go too fine,
       'With scarlet cloaks and bedgowns,
       'With velvet puggs and plaid-gowns,
       'With ruffled sleeves and headrounds,
          'More rich and gay than mine'.

'Forbear, proud madam Persian,
'Take back ye'r ain aspersion,
'Wi' tea, ye'r chief diversion,
          'Ye waste ye'r time awa:
'While dressing ye're and pinning,
'I'll spin, and bleach my linnen,
'And wear my ain hands winning,
          'Ye rector's lazy daw.

'I rise e'er the cocks craw day;
'My hands I spare not a' day,
'And wi' my farmer laddie
          'At night I take my ease:
'My husband plows and harrows,
'He sows and reaps the farrows,
'Shame fa' them wad change marrows,
          'For rector's gown and chaise.

'Sure some kind deel has brought us
'Yon yellow chiel[1] , that taught us
'To cleek the tythe potatoes
          'Frae ilk a greedy gown!
'Nae bishop, dean, or rector.
'Nae vicar, curate, proctor,
'Dare ettle now to doctor
          'Our skeedyines[2] under ground.

HE   Dear Madgie, e'en fairfaw ye!
     I'm blest that e'er I saw ye!
     A braid-claith coat I aw ye,
              Fac'd wi' a velvet cape:
     May milk and meal ne'er fail ye,
     May loss of yews ne'er ail ye,
     But geer grow on ye daily,
              For birking madam Crape

[1] The 'yellow chiel' was a lawyer, an enemy to the Established Church, who went by the name of 'Yellow Rowan'.
[2] small potatoes

That he might jockey horse.....

Simkin, or a Bargain's a Bargain - A Tale

Samuel Thomson (Commentary by John McIntyre)
ORIGINALLY PUBLISHED IN ULLANS NUMMER 4, SPRING 1996

The following poem is reminiscent of Burns's 'Holy Willie' and is a humorous account of an incident in which a hypocritical religious zealot tried to cheat an equally devious young twister over the sale of a horse, the eighteenth-century equivalent of a second-hand car deal. In the text printed below, all words that are italicised are defined to the right of the line.

Auld Sim [1] was fam'd for *prolix* prayers,	tedious, complicated
And *tuneful* [2] holy graces;	droning
Weel ken'd at markets, mills and fairs,	well known
And ither public places.	
A holy man - his conscience ne'er	
Wad suffer him to curse;	would
But saftly whisper'd in his ear,	
That he might *jockey* [3] horse.	deal, trade (his horse)
He held it as a *crying* [4] sin	scandalous
At *hame*, or *onie* place,	home; any
To *tak* a morsel, thick or thin,	take
Without a formal grace.	
This favorite o' Heaven *ae* day,	one
To a neighbouring fair wad *gang*:	go
Favourite of Heaven, did I say?	
Gude faith I'm *aiblins* wrang.	good; possibly, perhaps
Howe'er his *Bawsay* [5] to the fair,	old horse (a pet name)
Took crafty, *sleekit* Sim:	sly, cunning
A noble naig he did declare,	
But *didna answer* him.	didn't suit

Soon up there comes a *jockey chiel*,   horse-dealing man
Sim like a *Levite* ⁶ *winked* ⁷;   clergyman become corrupted
He tried the horse and lik'd him weel,
And soon a bargain *clinked* ⁸.   clinched

Quoth ⁹ Sim – 'although I say't mysel,   said
I'm reckon'd something clever *ay*;   always
We'll step in here an tak a *gill*,   measure of drink
An' then *yese* ¹⁰ get delivery'.   you shall

They call'd a gill, 'twas quickly there,
The *chiel* gets't in his *nieve* ¹¹,   lad; fist
When Simkin, with a holy air,
Says, 'stranger *wi'* ¹² yer leave'.   by

Thrice he *gov'd* up *niest* the roof,   gazed, looked intently; towards
As aften shook his head,
Then clos'd his *ein* ¹³, an' rais'd his *loof*,   eyes; palm
A holy man indeed!

The tricky *callan*, then, to keep   lad
Frae laughin scarcely *fit*,   from; able
Drank out the whiskey every *seep*,   dreg
And down the *bicker* set.   drinking-cup

The grace being done, the fellow *leugh*,   laughed
The whiskey was away!
To pray, *quoth* he, is not eneugh,   said
Hereafter watch and pray.

Delivery *gien* - they part *aff han*,   given; abruptly
So hame our nibour wan'ers:
Niest morn the *o'erseen* fellow *fan'*   next; outwitted; found
His gelding had the *glan'ers*!   glanders (a horse disease)

Neglecting to ask Simkin's name,
He's in an *eirie study*:   terrible fix
At length in passion aff he came,
Damning the praying body!

At lang and length he found the place,
Our Simkin's habitation;
Where entering in he *kend* his face,   recognized
And baul'd aloud - damnation!

Ye old infernal hound of hell!
Ye hypocrite deceiver!
A gland'red horse to me to sell -
Swith the money up deliver.   quickly

'*Hooly*', *quo* Simkin, *unco slee*,   just wait; said; very slyly
'*Gie o'er sic* sinfu' jargon;   stop such
Nae money ye shall get *frae* me -   no; from
A bargain's *ay* a bargain'.   always

---

[1] Sim, Simmie and Simkin are all Scots diminutives of the personal name Simon. However, 'Auld Sim' was also the equivalent of 'Old Nick', ie the devil.

[2] In Scots this can mean either 'speaking with pauses that don't make sense with what is being said' or 'with strength and feeling'.

[3] In Scots this can mean a horse-dealer or any sort of tramp-like trader. Thompson's use of 'jockey' as a verb meaning 'to deal or sell a horse' is otherwise unrecorded in Scots.

[4] Disgraceful, scandalous. In English, the only similar usage is with the phrase *crying shame*.

[5] *Bawsey* is a affectionate name for a horse and can also be used to mean any horse, as 'a Neddy' might be for a donkey.

[6] A contemptuous name for a clergyman, similar in meaning to 'Scribes and Pharisees'.

[7] In Scots *winkit* milk is turned sour. Here the meaning is 'corrupted or turned bad'.

[8] The meaning of literally gripping or clenching something is the only usage found in the dictionaries of Scots.

[9] Usually *quo* or *qo* in Ulster Scots.

[10] It is rare in Ulster Scots to find any use of *shall* rather than *will*.

[11] A related adjective, *nievefu* 'fistful', is the most common usage in Ulster Scots.

[12] An interesting example of the common use of this word equivalent to English *by*.

[13] The more usual spelling of this word is *een*.

A creepin heckle!

To A Hedge-Hog

Samuel Thomson, Carngranny, County Antrim, 1793
ORIGINALLY PUBLISHED IN ULLANS NUMMER 2, SPRING 1994

WHILE youthful poets, thro' the grove,
Chaunt saft their cranny lays o' love,
And a' their skill exert to move
      The darling object;
I chuse, as ye may shortly prove,
      A rougher subject.

What sairs to bother us in sonnet,
'Bout chin an' cheek, an' brow an' bonnet?
Just chirlin like a widow'd linnet,
      Thro' bushes lurchin;
Love's stangs are ill to thole, I own it,
      But to my hurchin.

Thou grimest far o' grusome tykes,
Grubbing thy food by thorny dykes,
Gudefaith thou disna want for pikes,
      Baith sharp an' rauckle;
Thou looks (L___d save's) array'd in spikes,
      A creepin heckle!

Some say thou'rt sib kin to the sow,
But sibber to the deil, I trow;
An' what thy use can be, there's few
      That can explain;
But naithing, as the learn'd allow,
      Was made in vain.

Sure Nick begat thee, at the first,
On some auld whin or thorn accurst;
An' some horn-finger'd harpie nurst
  The ugly urchin;
Then Belzie, laughin, like to burst
  First cad thee Hurchin!

Fok tell how thou, sae far frae daft,
Whar wind fa'n fruit lie scatter'd saft,
Will row thysel, wi' cunning craft,
  An' bear awa
Upon thy back, what sairs thee aft
  A day or twa.

But whether this account be true,
Is mair than I will here avow;
If that thou stribs the outler cow,
  As some assert,
A pretty milkmaid, I allow,
  Forsooth thou art.

I've heard the superstitious say,
To meet thee on our morning way,
Portends some dire misluck that day -
  Some black mischance;
Sic fools, howe'er, are far astray
  Frae common sense.

Right monie a hurchin I hae seen,
At early morn, and eke at e'en,
Baith setting off, an' whan I've been
  Returning hame;
But Fate, indifferent, I ween,
  Was much the same.

How lang will mortals nonsense blether,
And sauls to superstition tether!
For witch-craft, omens, altogether,
    Are damn'd hotch-potch mock,
That now obtain sma credit ether
    Frae us or Scotch fok.

Now creep awa the way ye came,
And tend your squeakin pups at hame;
Gin Colley should o'erhear the same,
    It might be fatal,
For you, wi' a' the pikes ye claim,
    Wi' him to battle.

For more of Thomson's poetry, see *The Country Rhymes of Samuel Thomson, The Bard of Carngranny, 1766-1840*, Vol. 3, The Folk Poets of Ulster Series, Pretani Press, 1992.

James Orr Memorial, Ballycarry, Co Antrim

The Penitent

(Inscribed to the Rev J Bankhead, Ballycarry - Written in the year 1800)

James Orr (Commentary by Philip Robinson)

ORIGINALLY PUBLISHED IN ULLANS NUMMER 8, HAIRST 2001

This is one of the finest poems by James Orr, the Bard of Ballycarry (1770-1816). It was written in the year 1800, just two years after Orr's participation in the '98 rebellion, and just after his return from a short spell in America as a fugitive. The poem tells the story of the downfall and redemption of a drunken weaver. In some senses it was a self-commentary, for Orr, himself a weaver, died in the same thatched house he had been born in 46 years before. His friend and biographer, A M'Dowell, said that Orr spent his last years in ill health, often fleeing 'the cheerless habitation of the bachelor, and was obliged to seek the pleasures of society at an inn'. But the religious controversies of the day were also meat and drink to Orr. In the almost exclusively Presbyterian district of Ballycarry, these controversies consisted primarily of the fierce debates between 'Auld Licht' Calvinism and the radical 'New Licht' Presbyterian intellectualism. Like so many of Orr's poems, 'The Penitent' was 'inscribed' to a Presbyterian minister of his acquaintance – in this case his own minister, the Rev. J Bankhead of Ballycarry. In the first nine stanzas of the poem, Orr describes Christy Blair as basically a decent but weak-willed weaver who had been taken to the brink of ruin by his inability to resist drink and base company. Then Christy goes to a local barn to pass an hour:

> ... Whare Smyth, the methodie, harang'd the folk:
>> They mourn'd an' cried amen – he fleech'd and fought,
> Christy grew grave, an' thought he'd join the flock,
>> An' imitate their lives wham ance he us'd to mock.

Although Methodists were as scarce as hen's teeth in Presbyterian east Antrim, Orr gives 'good old WESLEY' and 'Smyth, the methodie' the credit for Christy's conversion and reform. Clearly Orr was concerned to remove from his story any suggestion that he was simply an Auld Licht apologist. Indeed, in the last stanza he urges his fellow 'patriots brave, when we lie low in earth', to banish from Erin's shores 'religious wrath', and to follow 'Truth and Right, and guard the land they prize'. Apart from Orr's superb command of his native Ulster-Scots tongue, his vernacular poetry is characterised by sophisticated satire and metaphor. Another poem, 'Elegy on the Death of Hugh Blair, D.D.', gives us a tantalising suggestion of who 'Christy' Blair's reform exemplified. Rev. Dr Hugh Blair was Professor of Rhetoric at Edinburgh University, a leading exponent of the 'Moderate Party' in the Scottish Enlightenment and one of the most distinguished Edinburgh literati of the late eighteenth century. Significantly, Blair first introduced and promoted Robert Burns in Edinburgh Society after the publication of Burns' first book of collected poems in 1786. Blair died in 1800, the year Orr wrote both 'The Penitent' and his 'Elegy' to Hugh Blair. In the latter poem Orr describes listening to Blair's prophetic sermon:

> While fond to hear the far-fam'd foe of vice,
>   Amidst his audience pensively I lean'd,
> Sedate I saw him in the rostrum rise,
>   And heard him say with majesty unfeign'd –
>
> 'You shall I teach no more. The prize I reach;
>   'But lest you wander when my voice should cease,
> 'I've wrote my precepts that they still may teach
>   'An age to come, to follow truth and peace:

Returning to 'The Penitent', another clue to Orr's use in this tale of Christy Blair as an historico-religious metaphor is contained in the line: 'I learn'd his life frae Brice, the auld herd on the moor'. Brice, the old shepherd on the moor, could be none other than Rev. Edward Brice, the first Presbyterian minister to come from Scotland to Ireland and the father of Scottish Presbyterianism in Ireland. Brice came as minister to Ballycarry in 1612 and is buried alongside the monument to James Orr in Templecorran graveyard, Ballycarry.

'The Penitent' was re-printed in *Ullans* 8 (2001), in the context of that particular issue's theme of drink and drinking.

EARTH feels the triple scourge wild warfare spreads,
　　　Emaciate famine gnaws the husks and pines,
And ev'ry friend, forsaking, inly dreads
　　　The fated wretch, whom pestilence confines:
Say, will BANKFIELD, who piously declines
　　　Man's ev'ry vice, and mourns his woes severe;
Will he, the guide, who feels what he enjoins,
　　　The fervent love of ev'ry faith and sphere,
The Penitent's memoirs, tho' mean, be pleas'd to hear?

His name, if I min' right, was Christy Blair:
　　　Fu' aft I've pass'd the wa'-stead whare he leev'd;
An' auld ash tree stan's branchless now an' bare,
　　　Aboon the spring, unnotic'd an' unpreev'd:
The side wa' co'ers the causey that he pav'd,
　　　The beasts rub doon the cheeks o' ilka door;
Rank nettles the hearth on which he shav'd
　　　The nybers ance a week in years o' yore –
I learn'd his life frae Brice, the auld herd on the moor.

He weav'd himsel', an' keepet twathree gaun,
　　　Wha prais'd him ay for hale weel-handled yarn;
His thrifty wife an' wise wee lasses span,
　　　While warps and queels employ'd anither bairn;
Some stript ilk morn an' thresh'd, the time to earn
　　　To scamper wi' the houn's frae hill to hill;
Some learn'd the question-beuk in nyb'ring barn –
　　　Christy wrought unco close, whyles took a gill,
But when his wab was out had ay a hearty fill.

An' nae mean spunge was he; but wad hae lent
　　　Sums to poor sots, wha basely brak their word;
Rich rakes admir'd his sprie, sae weel he kent
　　　The way to heel, an' han', a guid game bird:
An' in the pit he wadna twice be dar'd,
　　　The odds were shamefu' when he cried 'fair play';
His nieve, that nail'd the messons to the sward,
　　　Wad stapt to lift their weanies frae his way:
He harm'd himsel' at times was a' that folk cud say.

But och! if vice the least indulgence claim
      'Twill wax, an' strengthen, like a wean at nurse;
Belyve he staid hale days an' nights frae hame,
      Tho' ae nights absence, ance he deem'd a curse;
An' aft brought hame nought but an empty purse,
      O' a' the hale wabs price he took to sell;
Then, sick niest day, poor Mary boost disburse
      Her pence, to get a glass his qualms to quell:
She grudg'd – he storm'd – the weans grat – hame grew hell.

At length he turn'd a doonright ne'er-do-weel,
      For ilka draught, he swore, but made him dryer;
The kye gaed baith for debt. A sorry chiel'
      Was he to cleave their stakes to men' the fire:
Mary ne'er min't the house – mair like a byre,
      But clash'd wi' nyber wives. Unkent to him
For tea, an' snuff, the troubled dame's desire,
      She'd smuggled meal an' seeds; tho' hunger grim
Devour'd the duddy weans, now in a wretched trim.

Gif ye had pass'd his door, ye'd either heard
      Him we his comrades madly makin' noise,
Or squabblin' wi' the wife. He seldom car'd
      To wake the looms mair profitable voice:
The weans were wicked mair thro' chance than choice,
      How marvellous wad been their mense an' grace!
He learn'd the lasses smut, an' gart the boys
      Drink dreadfu' toasts an' box for pence or praise;
They'd ca' their mother le'er, an' curse her till her face.

Whyles wi' his auld colleagues he blam'd his wife;
      He kent that she was slack, an' they were fause:
She sometimes took a drap, an' by the life
      A drinkin' wife's ay deem'd for greater flaws:
Ance when they differ'd, like a thoughtless ass,
      He listed wi' the sogers on the street,
Yet when he ru'd, wrang'd Mary pledg'd her braws
      To raise the smart money. To see her greet
Wad thow'd the hardest heart in army or in fleet.

Yet shame owrecam' him whyles, an' when advice
    Was properly applied it rous'd his pride,
He'd kiss the beuk, an' swear by a' the skies,
    He'd in nae change house drink till hallon-tide;
Then, then he thrave; but och! he cudna bide
    Frae worthless spen'thrifts, nor cud they frae him;
At first he'd drink his glass in some backside,
    But at the table when his brains 'gan swim;
When told o' a' niest morn he'd tremble ev'ry limb.

At lang an' last, when to the frightfu' edge
    O' dreary ruin, by his courses brought,
(For a' was gaen he had to sell or pledge
    The times were hard and nane would trust him ought)
To pass a painfu' hour, the barn he sought
    Whare Smyth, the methodie, harangu'd the folk:
They mourn'd, an' cried amen – he fleech'd and fought,
    Christy grew grave, an' thought he'd join the flock,
An' imitate their lives wham ance he us'd to mock.

An' change his life he did; the bull-beat came,
    He wadna gang; but ca'd it savage vice:
A serious nyber 'cause he stay'd at hame
    Gi'ed him a wab to weave, an' lent the price:
Late, late did he sit up, an' early rise,
    An' eat the bread o' care to get it weav'd;
Syne took it hame, gat meal, an' monie nice
    Auld claes, to thack the weans, we thanks receiv'd;
Somebody ay will help the poor an' weel-behav'd.

Nature a while, tho' thought forbearance hard,
    An' Habit, like a bough by force held straight,
Sprang till its ain auld thraw. When aff his guard,
    Twathree rash gills wad set him till't a' night;
An' much he'd said an' done that was na right:
    Ilk short relapse the clashes met to track o';
But practice soon made irksome trials light;
    As ane, at first, wha trys the pipe for lack o'
His health, halts, coughs, an' greus, yet *learns* to like tobacco.

While perseverin' in his heav'n-ward way,
      He lea's pale want behin', his cant' an' zeal,
Sae quite remarkable, mak' grave an' gay
      Laugh hearty at him, tho' they like him weel;
Has he a band to fill? he soon fin's bail,
      Nae pross ere plagues him now, sloth leas his hame;
He has baith kye an' corn, an' sells some meal,
      His frien's outbye add *mister* till his name;
An' alter'd Mary's now a douse an' dainty dame.

(Hail! good old WESLEY – this they owe to thee,
      The wise of all professions bless thy birth;
Believing what you taught, without a fee,
      'A poor way-faring man,' you ventur'd forth,
Striving where'er you went to free the earth
      From sin, enslaver of the human mind:
As godlike HOWARD, friend of woe an' worth,
      In many a realm consol'd the cells where pin'd
Poor persecuted slaves, kept there by kings unkind.)

Whase arm ance rash as Christy's? now tho' strong,
      Nae bangster tholes his nieve or sla-thorn black;
Wha ance blasphem'd like Christy? now his tongue
      Without minc'd oaths the lee-lang day can crack:
His nights ance spent with gamesters owre the pack
      Are pass't wi' deein' wights, or at his beuk;
The lyin' cash he ance wad sent to wrack,
      Lent, int'rest-free, sets up new-married folk –
He's far ower wise to jibe; but no owre grave to joke.

The weans and Mary kept the cottage neat;
      She was affectionate, an' fond were they;
They work't an' sang their hymns, and crack't, an' gree't,
      Fine was their speech, an' affable their way.
They werena stupes, wha fient na word can say
      For what they b'lieve; tho' first to rail an' rage
At a' wha differ. 'Mang some bolefu's mae,
      Ane *Fletcher's* warks, a bra unbias'd sage,
Gart' em wi' might an' mense the Calvinists engage.

An' searchin' for the truth improv'd their taste:
　　How nat'ral *Joseph's* life was weel they kent;
How *Moses'* muse her notes sublimely rais'd,
　　An' *Jeremiah's* deeply did lament;
The *spen'thrift son's* fine scene they weel cud paint,
　　An *guid Samaritan's* – an' nearer han',
How *Young* made night mair solemn wi' his plaint;
　　How *Milton's* eve was fair, his Adam fand;
How *Gray* was sad an' grave, an' *Shakespeare* wildly grand.

They min't baith warls. In warps boil'd by their han'
　　Did thrice ten shuttles lose their entrails sma';
An' on a scoup o' cheap, but mountain lan',
　　They graz'd yell kye, an' drain'd, an' lim'd the shaw.
Beasts, yarn, an' claith, aft call'd the sons awa';
　　The daughters wash'd, an' sew'd, an' span wi' care:
Christy did little, but directed a';
　　An' cute was he when unco folk were there;
For at the very warst he had baith sense an' lear.

'The e'e that saw them bless'd them'. Much they shar'd
　　Wi' frien's, wi' strangers', an' wi' a' in need;
Folk thought the fam'ly *fey* if e'er they err'd,
　　Bonnier an' better ne'er brak warls bread:
Christy ne'er strave to cross their loves; but gied
　　Mailin's, an' gear, to ev'ry lad an' lass,
He leev'd to train their weans, an' when he died,
　　Was what they ca' the leader o' a class –
Brice gied me this account, an' right weel pleas'd I was.

May my wild brethren turn to wisdom's path
　　An' grace poor Erin, plagu'd with want and dearth!
And banish from her shores religious wrath,
　　Desponding sloth, and dissipated mirth!
May sun-like Science from the poor man's hearth
　　Chase Ignorance, the owl that haunts the stys!
So patriots brave, when we lie low in earth,
　　'Harmless as doves, and yet as serpents wise,'
Shall follow Truth and Right, and guard the land they prize.

The Fechtin Dugs

by Robin Gordon (W G Lyttle)
ORIGINALLY PUBLISHED IN ULLANS NUMMER 4, SPRING 1996

[Editors' note: The following is an extract from the author's Robin's Readings, 1879.]

The Meer lukit at the megistrates, an' sez he –
'Wull yer honour purtect me frae this man?'
A pokit the Meer's coat tail. He lukit roon, an' sez he –
'Oh, Robin, A'm glad tae see ye, cum an' tak my place'.
Sez I, 'Sur, wull A get a wheen o' the polis tae stan' roon ye?'
A think he didnae hear me, fur he turned tae the megistrate agen, an' it micht hae been a lesson tae ignerant fowk the nice respectfu' wae he spauk. 'Yer honour', sez he, 'A'll hae tae gang hame, fur A'm no terble weel this mornin', but there's an auld gentleman here, a Mister Gordon, that can tell ye iverything. Treat him wi' ivery respect', sez he, an' wi' that he slippit awa oot o' the coort.
A polisman helpit me up intae the box, an' a returney man got up, an' sez he tae me, sez he –
'What dae you know aboot this case?'
'Weel', sez I, 'as A wuz gaun doon the street fur a bowl o' broth –'.
'Noo, dinna bother us wi' broth', sez he.
'Ye'll mebbe be gled o' a guid bowl o' them sum cauld day', sez I.
'Tell uz what ye seen', sez he.
'A saw a big bull-dug worryin' anither dug', sez I, 'jest as A wuz gaun fur a bowl o' broth', sez I.
'Confound yer broth', sez he, 'hoo big wuz the dug?'
'Oh', sez I, 'it wuz a brave big yin'.
'What size wuz it?' sez he.
'It wuz a guid lump o' a dug', sez I.
'Wull ye tell me hoo big it wuz?' sez he, gettin' cleen mad.
'Deed', sez I, 'it wuz as big as ony dug o' the same size iver A seen'.
'Whaur dae ye leev?' sez he.
'Doon in Bellycuddy', sez I.
'A think there's a guid wheen cuddies there', sez he.
'No as mony as A see here', sez I.
'Dae ye mean tae say that A'm an ass?' sez he.

'Weel', sez I, 'A hae as guid a richt tae ca' you an ass as you hae tae say A'm a cuddy; hooaniver, if the shoe disnae fit ye, why ye neednae pit it on'.

'Very good, my man', sez John Rea.

'Go on wi' yer story', sez the megistrate.

'Weel', sez I, 'the Meer axed that man there tae sayperate the dugs, an' whun he refused, then he said tae me that if A wud catch him by the heid he wud tak him by the tail'.

'Nonsense, man!' sez the returney, 'wha iver saw a man haudin' on by a dug's tail; yer thinkin' aboot cuddies noo'.

'Deed A em not', sez I, 'there's John Rea whun he's bathin' at the Pickey Rocks taks his big dug by the tail an' lets it poo him through the water'.

'Its a fact', sez John Rea, 'an' A'll not alloo this decent man tae be bulleyed'.

'Hae ye treveled much?' sez the returney man.

'A hae went ower a guid bit o' grun in my day', sez I, 'an' mebbe A hae seen as muckle as you hae'.

'Did ye iver see the Cleekypatra Needle?' sez he.

'Mony a time', sez I, 'oor Peggy keeps yin o' them tae dern my socks wi''.

The fowk gied a yell o' a lauch at that, an' sez John Rea, jumpin' tae his feet, sez he –

'A tell ye A'll no alloo this man tae be bulleyed'.

'Sit doon, sir', sez anither man, 'yer deleyin' the coort'.

'*Your* nae returney', sez John.

'A em', sez the tither, 'but you're a low unmennerly fellow, an' yer a ragin' bully, yer a –'.

A cudnae tell a' that wuz said. Five or six o' them wuz argeyin' an' yellin' through ither. The megistrate cudnae mak himsel' heerd, so he left the bench cleen disgusted. Then A saw the polismen winkin' an' lauchin' at yin anither, an' the fellows in the coort wur yellin' an' cheerin', an' as A saw naebuddy mindin' me, A slippit awa oot, an' startit fur hame.

That dug case cummed on agen a guid wheen times, an' the Meer sent me letters axin' me tae gang up an' gie evidence, but Peggy wudnae heer tell o' it. She said A had din plenty, an' that if A did won the case A wud get terble little thanks fur it, an' mebbe a guid dale o' abuse.

A tuk her advice, an' A beleev she wuz richt. Ivery time the Meer met me efterwards he lukit a weethin' dry wi' me'; hooaniver A didnae care, fur Am just as guid as he is. But frae that day till this Mister Mackerlane an' me haes been great freens. Mony a time,

whun A'm up in Bilfast, A call at his offis, an' mony a wee bit letter he haes writ fur me.
A maun tell ye sum day aboot the bathin' match him an' me had at Pickey Rock yin day.

Bab M'Keen on Things in General.

Bab M'Keen: The McKeenstown (Ballymena) Scotch Chronicler

by Stephen Herron

ORIGINALLY PUBLISHED IN ULLANS NUMMER 6, SPRING 1998

Bab M'Keen is perhaps one of the most unsung Ulster-Scots writers of national significance. He wrote for the *Ballymena Observer* for at least thirty years, from 1878 until at least 1910. He produced tens of thousands of words of material, from poems to a serialised history of England that took nearly a year to publish in full.

In one year alone – 1878 – there were 32 articles and letters written in Ulster-Scots from Bab M'Keen, mostly in the form of his regular column, 'Bab M'Keen on Things in General', wherein he discussed matters in the local and world news. His opinions and observations were usually wry and witty, using the voice of the Mid-Antrim farmer to make his points. In later years, he wrote at least as many articles, though there was a couple of years when his work did not appear at all. There was little that Bab M'Keen didn't write about. Every Twelfth of July he would cover the events that occurred: he referred to the celebrations, in one article, as the 'annual debate on Bigdrumology'. Some years on Halloween he would produce an article in theme with that holiday. One year his article described a 'spiritual experience' in the People's Park in Ballymena. The 'spirit' in question was probably purchased in a pub elsewhere in town. In this outing, as excerpted below, Bab speaks with the statue that still stands to this day. She gives him the benefit of her wisdom:

'Tell me the meanin' o' this Inthermediate Eddication', quo' I.
'Oh', quo' she, 'it's derived frae the deed languages, an'
signifies, jest middlin' at the best'.
'Hoo was it there was naebody went tae the train tae see Lord
Dufferin the ither mornin'?' quo' I.
'Jest because', quo' she, 'he was a guid man. If it had been yin o'
the Glesgow Bank Directors the folk wad hae sat up a' nicht tae
get a glowk at him. It's the wye o' the warl'.

Sometimes months would go by without an article from Bab M'Keen. This would not go unnoticed by the public, and Bab, upon his return, would often comment upon the concern shown, especially when it wasn't his fault that he had been gone so long:

> It's a guid lang while since I pit pen tae paper, an' 'deed the
> raison o' it was that I cudna get things prented when I did
> write. Some fouk can get the editor tae pit in whativer trash
> they sen'. Likely they hae some wye o' comin' roon him. But,
> as far as I was conserned, it was aye 'left ower for want o''
> space', or 'the subject was o' nae public importance', or it was
> 'a' balderdash', or some pit aff or anither. I got very angry wi'
> the editor, an' I jest threatened that if he wadna pit in a letter
> for me noo an' then I wad start a wee paper o' my ain, an' I
> think that broucht him tae his senses.

The previous statement was especially ironic, since it's likely that Bab was a nom-de-plume used by one of the editorial staff of the paper, possibly John or Robert Wilson[1]. But regardless of his actual identity, Bab M'Keen had a character of his own and had a long time to develop it.

Later, in 1889, Bab M'Keen wrote his 'History of England' nearly weekly. This was a fairly serious work, though it had Bab's unmistakable voice:

> The English spent the nicht in drinkin' an' singin' sangs, and
> the Normans at their releegious duties, an' the nixt mornin'
> they wur at it like sticks a breakin'. They foucht for six hoors,
> an' at the last Harold got a dab in the e'e wi' an arrow an' wus
> killed, an' at the same time his twa brithers fell, and William the
> Norman won the day an' the throne o' England.

The importance of this series of articles could be lost in the humour that pervades it. Such a literary work would be interesting enough, if it were not completely written in Ulster-Scots. To the best of my knowledge, no similar literary or historical work has appeared before in Lowland Scots or Ulster-Scots. The coherency of the work over the years lends itself to the belief that it was one writer producing the work, though the thought that there were others was also considered at the time[2]. Bab had a reply to those folk too:

> It has come tae my notish that there's some folk statin' that
> there's mair Babs than yin writin' for the Ballymena Observer.

Noo, if I hear ony mair o' it, there'll be tumblers for fower an'
bottles for twa more some o' these fine mornin's. Let folk be
wise the time, but there's only yin Bab, an he's M'Keen.

The sheer amount of material that Bab produced is impressive enough – probably
more than Archibald McIlroy and W G Lyttle combined, but spread over more than
thirty years. The humour and the intelligence within Bab's work is worthy of serious
consideration and now, a hundred years after he was in the prime of his writing,
perhaps he will get the recognition he deserves.

[1] Research into the subject has continued, and it is now known that Bab M'Keen was created by John Wier,
who was owner and editor of the *Ballymena Observer* newspaper from 1886 until 1927.
[2] When John Wier died, William Wier took over as Bab M'Keen until 1946, and his son Major Jack Wier,
continued the family tradition until 1970. See *Bab M'Keen: The Wit and Wisdom of an Ulster-Scot* (Ballymena:
Mid-Antrim Ulster Scots Society, 2002)

Dolly was hersel' a bit deef.

Dolly M'Croit

by Archibald McIlroy
ORIGINALLY PUBLISHED IN ULLANS NUMMER 1, SPRING 1993

[Editors' note: The following is an extract from the author's The Humour of Druid's Island, published in 1902.]

'Talk aboot the heathen abroad', said Geordie Eslor, one evening, to Staffy M'Crone, as they sat together enjoying a fireside 'crack'. 'Did ye iver hear tell o' the M'Croits?'

'Dae ye mean auld Jacky an' Dolly that leeved doon near the rockin'-stane?'

'The very same', Geordie replied, 'a think a mair ignorant couple could har'ly hae been foun' an' un'ner the sun'.

'So a hae been informed', Staffy answered.

'Auld Mr. McIntyre went tae visit them on yin occasion', Geordie continued, 'an' when he got inside the do'r, it tuk him some minutes afore he could see onythin' for the darkness an' peat-reek'.

'Jacky was deaf, an' was sittin' at his loom in a corner; on his heid a dirty nicht-cap, wi' an enormous tassel hangin' ower his ear; an' his face luck't as if it hadna seen sape or water for six months'.

'Jacky nether hear'd nor saw the minister's approach an' continued at his weavin'; but Dolly got up aff the creepy-stool on which she had been crouchin' ower the fire, snatched the 'cutty' frae her mooth, an' made a pretence o' drivin' the hens and ducks ootside, as weel as the soo which was gruntin' in contentment on the opposite side o' the fireplace, at the same time drawin' forrit a rickety chair for the minister'.

'Dolly was hersel' a bit deef; an' on that accoont, as weel as a dulness o' comprehension, she lost much o' the guid that Mr. M'Intyre did his best tae impart'.

'"The hoose abane?" she cried oot in response tae some remark he had made. "Why, it's no near as guid as whor we're sittin'; for it's just filthy wi' the hens and deucks"'.

'"But have you no idea", said Mr. McIntyre, "as to who it was that brought you from the land of Egypt and out of the house of bondage?"'

'"It couldna hae been us, yer rev'rence", says Dolly; "a was niver a mile ayont the Druid's Altar in my life, nor nether was Jacky"'.

'"Have you never heard", asked the minister, in despair, "of that place where there will be weeping and wailing and gnashing of teeth?"'

'"A hae only twa auld stumps left", says Dolly, "an they're no' fornenst ither"'.

The 23rd Psalm

ORIGINALLY PUBLISHED IN ULLANS NUMMER 2, SPRING 1994

The Psalms have been translated and paraphrased many times into Lowland Scots, and a few versions exist even in Ulster-Scots:

> The Lord bees ma herd for aye. A winnae hae want o ocht.
> He gars me lay doon in green pasture-laun,
> An airts me fornent the lown waters.

In fact, an anthology of some 20 versions of Psalm 23 in Scots was compiled and published in 1987 (*Psalm Twenty-Three: An Anthology*, compiled by K H Strange and R G E Sandbach). As far back as 1857, Henry Scott Riddell published *The Book of Psalms in Lowland Scotch from the Revised Version*, and his version of the 23rd Psalm is as follows:

Ane Psalm o' David
The Lord is my shepherd; I sallna inlak.
He mak's me til lye doun in green an' baittle gangs; he leeds me aside the quaeet waters
He refreschens my saul; he leeds me in the peths o' richteous-niss for his name's sak'.
Yis, thouch I wauk throwe the vallie o' the skaddaw o' deaeth, I wull feaer nae ill: for thou art wi' me; thy cruik an' thy staffe thaye comfirt me.
Thou prepairist me ane tabel in the preesince o' mine enimies: thou anaintist my heaed wi' oolie; my cupp rins ower.
Shurelie guidniss an' mercie sall follo me a' the dayes o' my liffe; an' I wull dwall in the hous o' the Lord forevir.

In 1871, P Hately Waddell published *The Psalms frae Hebrew intil Scottis*, a book which has been reprinted by Aberdeen University Press and is available today.

> The LORD is my herd, nae want sal fa' me:
> He louts me till lie amang green-howes; he airts me atowre by the lown watirs:
> He waukens my wa'-gaen saul; he weises me roun, for his ain name's sake, intil right roddins.
> Na! tho' I gang thro' the dead-mirk-dail; e'en thar, sal I dread nae skaithin: for yersel are nar-by me; yer stok an' yer stay haud me baith fu' cherrie.
> My buird ye hae hansell'd in face o' my faes; ye hae drookit my heid wi' oyle; my bicker is fu' an' skailin.
> E'en sae, sal gude-guidin an' guid-gree gang wi' me, ilk day o' my livin; an' evir mair syne, i' the LORD'S ain howff, at lang last, sal I mak bydan.

In 1924, William Wye Smith published another 'Braid Scots' version:

> The Lord is my Shepherd; my wants are a' kent; the pastur I lie in is growthie and green.
> I follow by the lip o' the watirs o' Peace.
> He heals and sterklie hauds my saul: and airts me, for his ain name's sake, in a' the fit-roads o' his holiness.
> Aye, and though I bude gang throwe the howe whaur the deid-shadows fa', I'se fear nae skaith nor ill, for that yersel is aye aside me; yere road and yere cruik they defend me.
> My table ye hae plenish't afore the een o' my faes; my heid ye hae chrystit wi' oyle; my cup is teemin fu'!
> And certes, tenderness and mercie sal be my fa' to the end o' my days; and syne I'se bide i' the hoose o' the Lord, for evir and evir mair!

Sam Allen from Killinchy has sent in this version of the 23rd Psalm in the Shetlandic tongue, as broadcast from the Muckle Kirk in Lerwick on 'Songs of Praise' in 1985.

Da Loard's my hird, I sanna want;
He fins me bols athin
Green modoo girse, an ledds me whaur
Da burns sae saftly rin.
He lukks my wilt an wanless cowl,
Stravaigin far fae hame,
Back ta da nairoo, windin gaet,
Fir sake o His ain name.

Toh I sood geng doon Death's dark gyill,
Nae ill sall come my wye,
Fir He will gaird me wi His staff,
An comfort me forbye.

My table He has coosed wi maet,
Whin fantin god da fremd;
My cup wi hansels lippers ower,
My head wi oil is sained.

Noo shorly aa my livin days
God's love sall hap me ower,
Until I win ta His ain hoose
Ta bide fir evermore.

In 1903, John Stevenson published *Pat McCarty, Farmer of Antrim, His Rhymes*. His version of the 23rd Psalm was as follows:

My Shepherd is the Lord, His hand
    Shall a' my wants supply;
In mony a green and pleasant land
    He mak's me doon to lie.
Alang the burn, the wimplin' burn,
    That bubbles ow'r the stanes,
He leadeth me roon' mony a turn;
    By right ways me constrains.
Tho' in the fearsome vale of woe
    I walk and see death near,
Thy rod and staff before me go,
    And tak' awa' my fear.
A table weel laid oot for me
    My ill-wishers see spreed;
My cup is brimmin' ow'r; by Thee
    Anointed is my heid.
Gudeness and mercy a' my days
    Shall surely follow me,
And ow'r my gratefu' heid always
    God's holy roof shall be.

More recently, our own Ernie Scott rendered the following version of 'The Good Shepherd' at a meeting of the Ulster-Scots Language Society in Ballyclare Town Hall in 1994:

Wha is my Shephard wel A ken
The Lord hisel is he
He leads me whaur the girse is green
An' burnies quaet that be
Aft times A fain astray wud gang
An' wann'r far awa
He fin's me oot, He pits me richt
An brings me hame an' a'
Tho' A pass through the gruesom sheugh
Fin' A ken that He is near
His muckle cruk wull me defen'
Sae A hae nocht tae fear
Ilk comfort whilk a sheep cud need
His thochtfu care provides
Tho' wolves an' dugs may prowl aboot
In safety me He hides
His guidness an' his mercy, baith
Nae doot wull bide wi' me,
While faulded on the fields o' time
His hame ma dwellin' be.

'A right pair are ye', quo' the PEDLAR, quo' he...

The Legend of Stumpie's Brae

by Cecil Frances Alexander

ORIGINALLY PUBLISHED IN ULLANS NUMMER 6, SPRING 1998

[Stumpie's Brae is outside Lifford in County Donegal. The following well-known poem was written in the Laggan dialect of Ulster-Scots by none other than Cecil Frances Alexander, the great hymn-writer of 'All Things Bright and Beautiful', 'There is a Green Hill Far Away', etc. This copy was sent in 'Frae a guid freen', Sandy Jack of Strabane.]

Heard ye nae tell o' Stumpies Brae?
Sit doon, sit doon, young freen,
I'll mak yer flesh tae creep the day,
An' yer hair tae stan' on enn.

Young man it's hard to strive wi' sin,
An' the hardest strife o' a'
Is where the greed o' gain creeps in,
An' drives God's grace awa'.

Oh, it's quick tae do, but it's lang tae rue,
When the punishment comes at last.
And we would give the world tae undo,
The deed that's done an' past.

Over yon strip of meadow land,
An' o'er the burnie bright,
Dinna ye mark the fir-trees stand,
Around yon gables white?

I mind it weel in my younger days,
The story yet was rife:
There dwelt within that lonely place,
A farmer an' his wife.

They sat the-gither all alone,
Ane blessed Autumn night.
When the trees without, and hedge, and stone,
Were white in the sweet moonlight.

The boys an' girls were gone doon all
A wee till the blacksmith's wake;
There pass'd ane onby the window small.
An' guv the door a shake.

The man he up an' open'd the door -
When he had spoken a bit.
A pedlar man stepped into the floor,
Doon he tumbled the pack he bore,
Right heavy pack was it.

'Gude save us aa', saes the wife, wi' a smile,
'But yours is a thrivin' trade'.
'Aye, aye, I've wandered mony a mile,
An' plenty have I made'.

The man sat on by the dull fire flame,
When the pedlar went to rest;
Close till his ear the Devil came,
An' slipp'd intil his breast.

He look'd at his wife by the dim fire light,
And she was as bad as he –
'Could we no murder thon man the night?'
'Aye, could we, ready', quo' she.

He took the pickaxe without a word.
Whence it stood ahint the door;
As he pass'd in, the sleeper stirr'd,
That never waken'd more.

'He's deid!', says the auld man, comin' back –
'What o' the corp, my dear?'
'We'll bury him snug in his ain bit pack,
Niver ye mind for the loss of the sack.
I've ta'en oot a' the gear'.

'The pack's owre short by twa guid span'.
'What'll we do?' quo' he.
'Och, you're a doited, unthoughtfu' man;
We'll cut him aff at the knee'.

They shortened the corp and they pack'd him tight,
Wi' his legs in a pickle hay;
Over the burn in the sweet moonlight,
They carried him till this brae.

They shovell'd a hole right speedily,
They laid him on his back –
'A right pair are ye', quo' the PEDLAR, quo' he,
Sitting bolt upright in the pack.

'Ye think ye've laid me snugly here,
An' none shall know my station.
But I'll haunt ye far, an' I'll haunt ye near,
Father an' son, wi' terror an' fear
Til the nineteenth generation'.

The twa were sittin' the verra next night,
When the dog began to cower.
And they knew by the pale blue fire light,
That the Evil One had power.

It had stricken nine, jist nine o' the clock,
The hour when the man lay dead;
There came to the outer door a knock,
And a heavy, heavy tread.

The old man's head swam round an' round,
The woman's blood 'gan freeze,
For it was not a natural sound,
But like some ane stumpin' o'er the ground
An the banes o' his twa bare knees.

And through the door, like a sough of air,
And stump, stump, round the twa.
Wi' his bloody head, and his knee banes bare
They'd maist ha'e died of awe!

The wife's black locks e'er morn grew white,
They say, as the mountain snaws,
The man was as straight as a staff that night,
But he stooped when the morning rose.

Still, year an' day, as the clock struck nine,
The hour when they did the sin,
The wee bit dog began to whine,
An the gaist came clatterin' in.

Ae night there was a fearfu' flood –
Three days the skies had pour'd;
And white wi' foam, an' black wi' mud
The burn in fury roar'd.

Quo' she, 'Gude man, ye need na' turn,
Sae pale in the dim fire light.
The Stumpie canna cross the burn,
He'll no' be here the night.

For it's o'er the bank, an' it's o'er the linn,
And it's up to the meadow ridge –'
'Aye', quo' the Stumpie, hirplin' in.
And he gie'd the wife a slap on the chin,
'But I cam' roun' by the bridge'.

And stump, stump, stump to his plays again,
And o'er the stools and chairs;
Ye'd surely hae thought ten women an' men,
Were dancing there in pairs.

They sold their gear, and o'er the sea,
To a foreign land they went,
O'er the sea - but wha can flee,
His appointed punishment?

The ship swam o'er the water clear,
Wi' the help o' the eastern breeze,
But the verra first sound in guilty fear,
O'er the wide, smooth deck, that fell on their ear,
Was the tappin' o' them twa knees.

In the woods of wild America,
Their weary feet they set;
But the Stumpie was there the first, they say,
And he haunted them on to their dying day,
And he follows their children yet.

I haud ye, never the voice of blood
Call'd from the earth in vain;
And never has crime won worldly good,
But it brought its after-pain.

This is the story of Stumpie's Brae,
An' the murderers' fearfu' fate.
Young man, yer face is turned that way,
Ye'll be gangin' the night that gate.

Ye'll ken it weel, through the few fir trees,
The house where they wont to dwell,
Gin ye meet ane there, as daylight flees,
Stumpin' aboot on the banes o' his knees
It'll jist be Stumpie himsel'.

Wullie's flail gets intae gear.

The Flail

by John Clifford (1955)
ORIGINALLY PUBLISHED IN ULLANS NUMMER 6, SPRING 1998

When winter firmly taks a houl',
And days are dreary, drab and coul',
Wi' bitter sleet and drivin' hail,
Then Wullie Boyd taks up his flail.

There's growin' stirks and milkin' kye
That need fresh fother by and by,
So Wullie's flail gets intae gear
And flings its echo far and near.

You'll hear him in the early morn,
Wi' steady thud he flails the corn.
He sees his beasts and horses fed
Afore his neighbours lea' their bed.

I've often watched wi' boyish glee
How Wullie made the barley flee.
I've heard the aged rafters croak
Beneath his steady, measured stroke.

See how the neat begirdled sheaf
Sae pink o' stem, wi' glossy leaf,
Succumbs tae Wullie's practised skill,
A sturdy human threshin' mill.

A swish, a thud, the flail descends,
The tortured sheaf in agony bends.
The seed is scattered roun' like hail
Neath Wullie's unrepentant flail.

Doon in the byre the drowsy kye
Are lyin' warm and snug and dry.
Unmindfu' o' the steady thud,
They doze content, or chew the cud.

At last the flail is cast aside,
The wooden hatch is opened wide,
The eager beasts soon understan'
That breakfast time is noo at han'.

And Wullie sees each gets its share,
A liberal feed wi' some tae spare.
And then the kitchen's temptin' smell
Invites him forth tae feed himsel'.

There's two big rashers, side by side,
A blue duck egg in gravy fried,
And fadge that tae your innards cling –
A breakfast fit for ony king.

Thus fortified, nae man can fail
Tae match the torture o' the flail,
For only sinews made o' steel
Can swing a flail - and swing it weel.

There's something noble, grand and rare
Tae see a flail swish through the air.
There's mystic music in each stroke
As though some tribal drum had spoke.

So nivermore will I complain
If through my bedroom window pane
The thud o' Wullie's flail should seep,
And spoil my early mornin' sleep.

Instead – I'll maybe breathe a prayer,
And think o' Wullie toilin' there.
But nivermore I'll be annoyed
Tae hear the flail o' Wullie Boyd.

He was drownded in a bog hole.

The Glaur

by John A Oliver
ORIGINALLY PUBLISHED IN ULLANS NUMMER 2, SPRING 1994

[Editors' note: The following short story, set in the late 1770s, is taken from John A Oliver's book Girl, Name Forgotten … Stories from Seven Centuries of Family History, published by Littlewood Press, 1991, and is reproduced here by permission of the author. It contains dialogue written in the north Londonderry dialect of Ulster-Scots found along the Magilligan foreshore of Lough Foyle.]

'What's that ye're dae'n, Meta? Ye'll be destroyin yersel entirely, so ye will. If ye hauch ony mair on that bit o glass ye'll be stairtin tae skelly'.

'I've got a shilcorn an I'm trying tae dig it oot'.

'Ye'll mak a quare midden o yer face, for ye'll end up wi a beelin couter, I'm tellin ye'.

'I'm ga'in tae tak a race up tae the Big Drain Brig the nicht an I cannae face the ither cutties wi a big black shilcorn on me neb'.

'An what are you fossickin for Minnie?'

'I'm lukin for the reddin comb, Ma. I'm ga'in wi her tae the Brig. Where's the comb, Ma?'

'It's thonder, by the chimbley, daughter. It's fell aff the salt box an is lyin undher the oul thraw-heuk. But what dae ye be needin a comb for?'

'My hair's a fanked, so it is. I maun redd it oot'.

'An who'll be lukin at a lass like you, wud ye tell me?'

'There'll be a lot o the lads at the Brig. A the lasses dae their hair up. I'm quare an hungry, Ma, I want somethin tae ate'.

Looking at her two big girls Tillie Shearer could not help noticing, as she always did, how alike they were in appearance even if they got on badly together: plump and well-covered, fair, blue-eyed, pink-cheeked with broad open countenance. Like all the Shearers they'll be good breeders, Tillie assured herself. Meta claimed to be worried by the hint of red in her hair but Tillie knew it was only to be expected; it came from her side; most of the Conns were red. It gave a girl something extra, Tillie thought.

Tillie went on: 'I'm still waitin for yer Da and Jamie tae come back. I'm startin tae wonder what's kapin them'.

'What hae ye got for us tae ate, Ma?'

'Naethin, Meta, naethin but poundies. That's a. Nae kitchen'.

'That'll be a wersh bite'.

'Yous can throw in a gropin o scallions'.

'I hate scallions. They make me quae-wake. Is there nae rabbit?'

'Isn't it aboot time yous big girls were makin the meals yersels? Luk oot the door. I seen wee Andy deukin past. He's yer rabbit-ketcher. He's afeerd tae come in. Andy!' and she let a big gulder out of her. 'Andy, did ye ketch mony rabbits, son?'

'Naw, nane, Ma. I cannae dae it. An this pup Prince is nae help. It taks Jamie an the collie bitch. Jamie's great at the ketchin. I nearly ketched wan, but'.

At that their neighbour from over the march fence, Edward Clyde, came in the door with a heavy bucket in his hand.

'Guid day tae yous a. Here's a wheen o flukes for yer dinner'. There was never a more welcome caller than Edward at any time. Everyone crowded round. Edward could be counted on to be generous with whatever he had. 'Can ye spare them? There's a lot in that bucket. Don't ye need them for sellin?' And so on flowed the simple questions.

'I hae eneuch', he answered in his slow friendly speech. 'I hae eneuch, bairns. We brought in a gran ketch this morn. The Moville men werenae oot. I allow it's some class o a holyday in their kirk – so we had baith the nearder bank an the furder bank tae owersels. We had Lough Foyle tae owersels last nicht, ye might say. We had lashins and lavins – mair nor Martha Forebis wud tak frae us for his place. Ony way, these are naethin but the drachlins, so yous are welcome tae the lot', he added in his self-deprecatory style. But everyone, even the children, could see through his harmless blaflum, for these were perfect specimens of fully-grown flounders.

'Where's yer man, Tillie?'

'He's awa up on the turf mountain wi Jamie. This'll be their first draw o the turf this saison. It'll be guid an dry after these wheen o days o fine weather, but I doubt they've left it a bit late. I'm afeerd this weather'll no last. I cud hear the souch o the waves an the Back Strand the day, an that's aye a bad sign. When we get the turf I'll see that ye get a wheen o the best, Edward, forenenst the flukes'.

'There's nae need tae be calculatin that way Tillie. But I admit I cud be dae'n wi an armful o guid hard black peats. I hae naethin left frae last year but a clatter o oul fozie clods. Maybe Jamie cud bring some ower wan avenin'.

'Tam hasnae brought me ony sweeties the day. Where's Tam? What's kapin him?' This was the Granny from the fireside.

'What are ye skraikin aboot noo, oul woman? Dinnae be sae daft. Tam's been awa for years an years in Americay. Ye're dotin again, Granny. Oor men ought tae be here noo, I dinnae ken what's holdin them. They borrowed Canice O'Cahan's new scotch cairt – it's handier an quicker nor oors. Minnie, Minnie! What are ye dae'in? Put a hippin on that wean, wud ye, like a guid lass, she's ga'in tae kak again. She's got the scour, quick, daughter. Ye can see for yersel that she's dwammie. She's sickenin for somethin'.

'There's a lot of wrack on the foreshore', said Edward, disregarding that little domestic interruption. 'It luks the best o stuff. Yous cud be rakin it up for Jamie and yer Da tae cairt back tae the midden. Meta, Minnie yous are a pair o sonsie big weemen noo. That's somethin useful yous cud be dae'in for yer Da. I cud show yous the handiest way tae stairt, wi a rake an a graip'.

'She's nae guid at ony class o work. She's a useless big gamphrel, so she is. I wudnae work alangside her'.

'But ye'd traipse up tae the big Drain Brig behind me, fast eneuch, wudn't ye?'

'That's different, but. I like workin wi Jamie but I hae wrought in the harvestfield wi her an she's a fouter. An she's clootie, forby'.

'She's aye gettin in my road, so she is', giving her sister a dunt.

'Is it naw time yet for my breakfast?' came from Granny in her corner.

'Granny, dear, ye're wrang in the heed. It's far past middle-day. Meta, warm up some o them brochan an gae them tae yer Granny in a sup o milk. Shoosh, it's that ould mangy cat again. She has her heid in the milk. Shoosh, awa wi ye! Luk, weans, the pissmouls is in again. Meta, Minnie, Mary, whatever yer name is, get the whisk an sweep them oot. I cannae stand them in the hoose. They give ye hives, so they dae'.

'Far waur nor the pissmouls', said Minnie as she advanced on the ants. 'The clocks is back. They're climmin up the wa's'.

'Aye that's a terrible bad sign', responded Tillie. 'Get them oot! Get them oot!'

'Did I see yous the ither avenin, childer, tryin tae lep ower the sheugh?' asked Edward in his friendly, teasing way. 'I happened tae be dandherin ower tae a ceilidh in the Colquhouns an the Buchanans – we're a freends throughither, ye ken – an I was keekin at ye through the benweeds and the big bracken. Yous werenae makin a guid job o it, were yous? Did wan o yous fa in?'

'That was me', confessed Andy. 'I nearly lept it, but the broo o that Drumahorgan sheugh is higher on the wan side nor the ither. Jamie can lep it. Jamie's great at leppin, an he's larnin the collie bitch tae lep, forby, baith ways, so he is'.

'I maun be gettin hame tae my ain fireside and mak mysel a bite an a sup', Edward announced modestly.

Tillie rose, folding her arms, and convoyed him as far as the sally bushes by the stack-garden. 'That's a lovely avenin', said Edward self-consciously as they walked slowly along. 'Jist luk at that September sun ga'in doon ower Donegal, shinin aff the sandy hills and the ripenin barley. "Count yer mony blessings, name them wan by wan" I say to mysel on an avenin like this, Tillie'.

Tillie paid no attention to the scenic beauties. 'Jamie's growin up to be a grand lad, Edward. He's gettin more an more like you every day'.

'I'm glad, Tillie, I'm glad. I know ye're mighty proud o' him'.

'An Master Morrison tells us that Jamie's a gran scholar, forby – the smairtest scholar he ivver taught in the Margymonaghan school'.

'I'm glad, Tillie, I'm glad. I'm terrible glad. I'd like Jamie tae come on the boat wi us. Jacob an me, we cud be dae'in wi anither pair o hans. I cud larn him the fishing. It's a hard life an a lonely wan but it's a gran way o livin wi nature, wi the sky an the stars an the tides and the currents, livin close tae God himsel. A gran life'.

'Joe's no larnin him muckle at the fairmin. Joe's nae fairmer. It was wrang o him tae bide on the fairm. He'd a been far better at the schoolteachin or the claerkin. This fairm's ga'in tae rack an ruin. Luk at thon field o' barley ower the sheugh an the big field o oats beyont the sannyhole. The barley's mair than ripe and Joe hasnae aven stairted tae cut it. An when he daes stairt, he'll be hackin at it wi a wee bill-heuk nae bigger nor yer han. He hasnae got a scythe. An there's Alec McCracken wi wan o them new reapers. I allow that's what they ca them. But I nivver mismake mysel. I jist say tae mysel that Tam Shearer wud hae been better tae bide on the fairm here instead o emigratin. But he thought it was up to him tae laive the place for his brother an mak a new life for hissel in the new world'.

'I ken, I ken', said Edward soothingly. 'Tam wanted tae be upsides wi the ither lads that were emigratin at that time. The Meenister was tellin me a while back that half the lads in oor kirk went in them ten years or so – he has been reckonin it oot tae tell the Presbytery'.

Changing her tone and stance abruptly Tillie suddenly said: 'I can hear the cairt comin noo. It makes a big brattle comin ower the bit o stoney causey at Joshua McCracken's place. Guidbye, Edward'.

'Guidbye, Tillie'.

Across the flat treeless plain of Magilligan a horse and cart could be seen from a far distance.

'I can see my Da but I cannae see Jamie', Meta called from where she stood on a small dung-hill.

'He maistly runs alangside'.

'The cairt's empy. There's nae peats in it'.

'Somethin's wrang. Good God in Heaven, somethin's wrang'.

'Where's Jamie? Where's my wee Jamie? Joe, what's wrang? Where's Jamie?'

Joe walked over and hugged Tillie close to him, close and long. He could hardly get the words out and yet he stumbled on, blurting out one bit of his story after another.

'You've been drinkin, Joe. I can smell it aff ye, so I can. What hae ye been dae'in?'

'He's gone, Tillie. Jamie's gone. He was drownded in a bog hole. I didnae richt see what happened. I was awa frae oor bink – just for a wee minute – talkin tae Willie Doherty's wans up on the higher ground where their new bink is an I was pointin oot the hills o Scotland tae them – they ken naethin, them Doherty boys, – Kintyre, Islay, the Paps o Jura. Ye see, there was a bit o north in the wind, Tillie, an the air was terrible clear an …'

'What happened, man, what happened? Tell me quick'.

'I cudnae help it, Tillie, I swear tae ye I cud nae help it. Jamie was larnin the collie bitch tae lep over the bog water on tae the next bink. It seems it was boste and caved in. Jamie stummled. The dogue got awa'.

Meta and Minnie fell silent as they saw their brother's lifeless body on the floor of the empty cart, with a couple of bags thrown over it.

'Jamie sank intae the bog hole, the deepest hole in oor moss, frae wan en tae the ither. He was sprauchlin somethin terrible when we got there. He got stuck in the black glaur. I did my best, Tillie, but I cudnae pull him oot. The black water closed ower his heid, Tillie. I'm tellin ye, it tuk ten men, at the hinneren, the Quigleys and the McLoughlins an the Doherty boys, wi spades an ropes an planks, tae dig Jamie's wee body oot o the glaur'.

A schip pit oot fae Loch Fergus.

Tha Earn Wäng
(The Eaglewing)

by John Erskine
ORIGINALLY PUBLISHED IN ULLANS NUMMER 3, SPRING 1995

Mair nor thie hunner an fäftie yeir syne, in 16 an 36, a schip pit oot fae Loch Fergus (Belfast Lough) intil tha narra wattèrs o tha Dalriadae Sey atweesh Ulstèr an Scotlann an oot intil tha wattèrs o tha Atlaintic. Thar wes yin hunner an fowrtie fowk abuird tha schip an thai haed ettlet tae quät Ulstèr an tae flit til tha new worl, til Americae. Bot twa munt efter, tha schip, gey blathert an tha fowk fair forfauchen bot muckle blythe tae gat aisement, pit in yinst mair til Loch Fergus. Thai haenae wun owre.

Sae, quha wud aa thir fowk hae bin, an quhitfor haed thai ettlet tae flit til tha new worl?

A Hairtsair Fowk

Thae days wus gey an haird an a hairt-scad for tha Scotch Presbyterians in Ulstèr: thai wernae weel thocht o an wer aa ill-houden bi tha Athorities. Quhan Wentworth wes appunct Laird Depute o Airlann he cudnae thole tha Presbyterians. Wentworth an tha pralats, abies Ussher, turnt agin tha Presbyterians an huntit tha männystèrs frae thair maetin hooses. Tha Scotch in Ulstèr wes taen fer rebels – nae bischop, nae käng, jaloused Wentworth – an thai cudnae worschip tha Lord thair ain gate forebye hidlins in thair hames an oot hooses an on tha braes. Thai haed muckle wrocht wi tha heich heidyins bot nae guid cum o it ava. Thai cudnae dae ocht mair an thai cudnae thole it nae langr. Monies tha yin wes mindit tae flit til Scotlann: thai cudnae bot, acause tha Presbyterians wes ill-houden thar an aa.

A wheen o fowk foregaithert fer a collogue an yin o tha kenspeckle männystèrs, John Livingstone, scrievit in 16 an 34 til John Winthrop, Governer o Massaechusetts, speirin at him gin thar wudnae be onie lann fer tae be haed in New Inglann. In thae days monies tha Puritan fae Inglann wus flittit til Americae: tha Pilgrim Faithers haed pit oot in tha Mayflooer in 16 an 20, a wheen o yeirs afore. Winthrop wes hairtenin til thaim an affert lann til thaim on tha braes o tha Merrimac Wattèr.

A Schip Gets Biggit

Tha fowk, gey upliftit bi tha wittins, ettlet tae flit til New Inglann an wes mindit tae fynn tha haun o tha Lord in it aa. Thai gart a schip be biggit, a schip o 115 ton, aiblins at Groomsport, bot mair like at Cairrick. Thai cried tha schip Earn Wäng (Eagle Wing) fae tha wuirds in tha Buik o Exaedus (19:4).

Ye hae saen wi yer ain een quhit A daen til tha Aegyptians an quhitwey A hae uphouden ye on earn's wängs an brocht ye here tae masel.

Tha fowk had ettlet tae pit oot in tha Spräng, quhan tha wather wud hae fairit an weel afore tha blufferts o tha hinnerenn o tha yeir. Bot thai beed tae wait on tha schip gettin biggit an ootreikit: thai didnae quät thair hames tae tha simmer. Thai selt thair hames an aa thai haed an gat thairsels buskit fer tha traik. Thai wer gey an riz, bot thai wur vext tae quät tha pairts an tha freens at thai kent forebye. In amang tha fowk – menfowk, weeminfowk an childer, tha feck o thaim frae Ulstèr bot a wheen frae Scotlann forebye – wus tha männystèrs Robert Blair an John Livingstone an tha Provost o Ayr, John Stuart. Thai haed muckle lippenins in thair hairts.

Tha Schip Pits Oot

Tha schip pit oot fae Cairrick on tha 9t Sectemmer an tuk til tha narra seys atweesh Ulstèr an Scotlann airtin til tha north. Bot quhaniver scho pit oot intil tha narra seys scho cum on frowart wuns at driv her intil Loch Ryan tae hiddle. Quhan tha wuns wes lown scho pit oot yinst mair. Scho haednae gat faur tae scho pit in til tha Kyles o Bute acause tha timmers wus lattin in. Thai groondit her tae colf tha timmers an tae mak her calfat. Bot bi Robert Blair's wye o't it wesnae tha schip bot tha hairt o tha chaptane at wus fushionless. Scunnert wi aa his taiglin tha fowk walet anither boadie fer tae be chaptane.

Fash Oot in tha Atlaintic

Yinst mair thai pit oot intil tha Atlaintic. Tha wather wes fordèrsome an tha schip snoved thie or fower hunner league wioot onie fash. Bot quhan thai cum mair inby Newfunlann nor Euraip tha wather gat waur. A bluffert frae tha north an west gat up an stairtit tae gurl an skirl an hushle tha graith. It cum a blouster an dingit tha schip. Scho wes jachelt an scho howdit an wus aa bot whammelt wi tha sey. Tha wun rivit tha foresaile an smathert bäts o tha graith. Tha waws hovit an cum in owre tha schip an owre tha cahute an aa; thai bruckit doon yin o tha gran simmers an dingit tae scowes a wheen o tha clifts o tha owreloft an drookit aa tha fowk at wes atweesh tha lofts. Tha schip stairtit tae tak in an thai haed tae yuise twa pomp tae pit oot tha wattèr.

Waur nor aa thon bot, tha bensell o tha blouster dingit tha gubernakil fae tha huidins an thai cudnae airt tha schip ava. Yin o tha fowk, Andra Agnew, wi a cordell pit roon him an wi his lumes lappit til him, wes pit doon owre tha side an wi nae mair nor his heid abune tha wattèr wrocht tae he haed it couthert.

Bot tha chaptane an tha menfowk o tha kippage cum tae tha fowk an telt thaim at thar wes mair blousters an mair fash tae cum an threapit at in tha hinnerenn o tha yeir thai cudnae haud wi aa tha frowart wather. Thai wud hae til pit aboot an mak a hame-cumin in Ulstèr yinst mair.

Tha Schip Pits Aboot

Tha fowk wes gey forfauchen bi quhit thai wer telt bot jaloused at aiblins tha blouster wes brocht bi tha Lord an at He haednae ettlet for thaim tae gang til Americae ava. Aiblins He haed ettlet fer thaim tae wark in Ulstèr an Scotlann. Thai wer mindit tae bide fower an twonnie hoor mair. Gin tha blouster wes lown efter fower an twonnie hoor thai wud thole tha wather an luk tae win tae Americae, bot gin tha blouster haednae lowdent efter fower an twonnie hoor thai wud tak it fer a taikin frae tha Lord, wud pit aboot and mak a hame-cumin in tha kintra thai haed quät. Tha blouster daednae lowden. Tha schip pit roon an makkit for tha aist. Tha wather wes fordèrsome an at lenth an lang, roon aboot 3d Novemmer, tha schip pit intil Loch Fergus yinst mair.

Tha traik wes a sair hairt-scad on tha fowk: an auld bodie an a wean deed and wus pit owreboord an tha day efter tha hame-cumin, William, at wes tha bairn o Robert Blair, deed forebye. On tha traik, tha guidwife o Michael Colvert cleckit a wean at Mr Livingstone kirstent 'Seaborn'. Thai haed muckle tholet. Thai wer forfauchen an thai wer feart at ither fowk wud scrip thaim. Bot in thair hairts thai tuk it fer certes at it wes tha Lord at haed gart thaim pit aboot an haed brocht thaim tae Loch Fergus yinst mair. Tha fash o tha lang dreich sailin wes by thaim an thai jaloused at tha Lord haed ettlet on ither darg fer thirsels. An in tha incumin yeirs a guid wheen o tha fowk at haed pit oot in tha Earn Wäng wud chaave owre ocht fer tha Scotch an tha Kirk in Ulstèr an Scotlann.

Quhit wud hae bin tha wye o't gin thai haednae pit oot at tha hinnerenn o tha yeir, bot? Quhit wye wud thai hae bin gin thai haed wun tae Americae? Quha kens? We cud gang intil tha moyens o't. In tha owregate o't, tha traik o tha Earn Wäng misgaed. Tha fowk daednae wän owre. Hooaniver, we maun gie respeck tae, an ferlie at, thae fowk at ettlet at bein wor ain Pilgrim Faithers lang syne.

Notes on spellings: There is no fully accepted style of writing and spelling Ulster-Scots. This text represents simply one approach. Certain, slightly modified, standard forms of written Scots are used here: *tha* 'the'; *thae* 'those'; *thai* 'they'; *thaim* 'them'; *thair* 'their'; *thar* 'there'; *thir* 'these'. The traditional Scots form 'quh-' is retained where 'wh-' would be used in English.

Glossary:

abies – except

ahint – behind

aiblins – perhaps

Airlann – Ireland

airt – to steer

aisement – relief

appunct – to appoint

atweesh – between

beed tae – had to

bensell – violence (of a storm)

big – to build

blather – to beat, pummel

blouster – violent squall

bluffert – squall of wind and rain

blythe – glad, happy

bruckit – broke

buskit – prepared

cahute – ship's cabin

calfat – waterproof

certes – certain

chaptane – captain

cleck – to give birth to

clift – plank

colf – to caulk, fill

collogue – private discussion

cordell – rope

couther – to mend, repair

cried – called

darg – work, task

ding – to beat, batter

ding tae scowes – to smash to pieces

drook – to drench, soak

earn – eagle

efter – after, afterwards

ettle – to plan, intend

fair – to improve, clear up

fash – trouble, bother

ferlie – to wonder, marvel

fordèrsome – favourable

forfauchen – exhausted, worn out

frowart wuns – contrary winds

fushionless – lacking strength

gang intil the moyens o' – make inquiries about

gar – to cause, make

gin – if

graith – rigging

groond – to ground, beach

gubernakil – rudder

gurl – to roar, howl

hairtenin – encouraging

hairtsair – vexed, heartsore

hairt-scad – source of grief

hinnerenn – latter part

hovit – rose

howd – to pitch up and down

huidin – hinge

hunt – to drive out, expel

hushle – to blow in gusts, blow through

ill-houden – oppressed

in the owregate o't aa – when all's said and done

jachelt – buffeted

jalouse – to suspect

käng – king

kenspeckle – well known

kippage – crew

kirsten - to christen
lappit – tied
lattin in – leaking
lenth and lang – (at) long last
like – likely
lippenins – hopes, expectations
loft – deck
lowden – to die down, diminish
lown – calm, diminished
lumes – tools
maist feck – greater proportion
misgae – to fail
monie – many
munt – month
narra seys – narrow sea, strait
ocht – anything
ootreikit – fitted out
owreloft – top deck
owre ocht – very much
pralat – prelate
respeck – admiration
rivit – tore
riz - excited
sair – distressing, oppressive
scrip – to mock
selt – sold
simmer¹ – summer
simmer² – beam, spar
skirl – to blow with a shrill noise
smather – to smash, shatter
snove – to move steadily
speir at – to ask
syne – ago

taiglin – delay
taikin – token
threap – to argue strongly, assert
tofruschit – smashed to pieces
traik – journey, voyage
uphoud – to support, uphold
vext - sorrowful
wale – to select, choose
wäng – wing
waur – worse
waw – wave
wede – to rage
whammelt – overturned
win – to reach (a destination)

Madge Thompson (with grandsons Graeme and Mark Thompson), Ballyfrench, c. 1975

A Bricht February Mournin

by Mark Thompson
ORIGINALLY PUBLISHED IN ULLANS NUMMER 7, WUNTER 1999

We cairryt her
Doon tha brae by tha fiel whaur we kepp tha beess
Dizens o fowk ahin us forbye,
An tears wallin up in ma een.
Past tha enn o Skelly's road an by Sam Beggs's loanen
Tha wun wus coul on Bellyfrench
Thon bricht February mournin
A wheen o fiels an a dizen o hens
She spent her days leukin efter
It gien her hauns somethin tac dae
Amang tha tears an tha lauchter
A hae mynn o tha day she wus bakin
Her shoartbreid wus burnt
A filled ma pokits
Wi black shoartbreid
Feart
Ma granny micht greet
We taen her tae Bellyhailbert
An laid her alangside her man
Whaur he wus waitin foarty-echt year
Leukin ower tha Sheugh tae Scotlann
A miss her
Whiles
A quair wee woman she wus
Bot A'll see her yin day
An ma granda forbye
A'll tell her o aa tha fuss
She gien us whun she left,
As intil tha grun she wus lowerin
An we happed her ower wi flooers an tears
Yin bricht February
Mournin.

Rinnin wae the Maine Watter

The Flow

by James Fenton
ORIGINALLY PUBLISHED IN ULLANS NUMMER 5, SIMMER 1997

The flow's ower nixt Dunloy, a smal pairt o the lang wat boags rinnin wae the Maine Watter frae the Broonstoon tae Brig-en, whar yintim a lock o yins cut the wunter's peats. Sitch stur wuz thonner, wae a guid simmer, frae Mie on, frae the furst scra-parin tae the dra'in or dreggin wae coaglin cairts oot the slunky rodden. Maistly in twas or threes they wrocht, at their ain bink, quait maistly, wae the cutters leengin at the breesht an the wheelers half-rinnin, kempin, tae stie wae them; tae they gethered thegither, brockie-faced wae sweet an peat, tongues an baks crakkin baith, an taen their pieces, wat wae tay as blak gyely as the moss-watter itsel. Sae mony then, sitch stur, but naw noo; al's quait noo, naw a yin aboot. (An mair nor that's quait, awa, or maistly sae. Sae weel ye mine it: the whaps an the peeweeps an their lachters jookin, the crakin frae the yella star on the heecher grun, the tittle foriver efter the cryin gowk, an whutrets keekin an wheekin ooty the staks o owl peats; an aye gin dailygan the enless bizzin o thon wee burd amang the seggans an queelrods, the yin ye hard but niver sa.)

An mae fether: breeshtin wuz his wie, the wie o maist, the wie whar the bink wuznae ower heech, the big en o them in thon sapplin moss – a gullion wae a wat start – wae a brev lair o fog an fum taen aff the binkheid. The odd yin stanked, but naw mony; an the only untherfittin wuz whar, for yince, the bink ruz weel abain the shoother. (Ower bae Slaimish, bae the Vogey side, it's whiles the ither wie roon: untherfittin – trinkctin, they ca it – is the only wie wae the peat a shella lair.) Breeshtin: an mony's the lang, sore evenin oor he wrocht at it, efter a' the ither oors. An's aye thonner, sae weel ye see him: plowterin in the fit-ga, simmet appened doon, galluses hingin, sweet lashin, the twarthy tails plestered flet tae the gowpin croon, teeth gruppin the unther lip an een bleezin as he driv at the bink. (An seein him thon wie noo, ye mine, tae, a wain's wuntherin whun owl Dinnis, sweetin an sweerin an reekin whuskey, towl him Davy Leary had a machine tae dae it.)

An yersel, a gral o a weefla, kilt wheelin tae him. For wheelin ower wat grun wuz a wexer, an copin on the wunnin grun wuz knakky enugh: brek them, an a' ye'd hae at the hinther en wud be a bing o clods an a lock o coom – as a rair frae the bink wud aply mine ye.

Nae sweerin wae mae fether; but a doag in the breesht raised him mair nor a weethin. A big akward doag – naw lake cat (doldrum, up the country), shoart an tyugh, that gien some o iz a ra, jooked reek whun wun, but the butt o a tummock, or a hale tummock, biried in the moss frae wha knows whun – brocht the cuttin tae a stap.

Hokin it oot wuz a sizzem (anither boady wud 'a swore) an made a wile hashter o the face; but the wheeler, quait, got his wun.

The wunnin itsel wuz naethin: fittin an castlin an ricklin taen naethin ooty ye (bar whutiver the midges taen). An the oany bother wae cairtin hame wuz thon rodden, slunky an stoory or slunky an wat, but slunky aye, whar lairin or copin, wae ower mony on, wuz a rail chance. Sae ye'd maistly hae tae hal oot in dregs, heelin up yin dreg on the road bunker tae be clodded an bigged on the nixt, tae mak a hale laid for hame.

Nor thocht the yin, micht loass the tither...

Minin Bab

by James Fenton
ORIGINALLY PUBLISHED IN ULLANS NUMMER 5, SIMMER 1997

We sa the licht a fiel apairt,
Wur niver lang frae ither;
We progged for fun in ivery nyuck,
An fun the diel thegither.
Nor thocht the yin
Micht loass the tither.

For enless oors alang the lade
An doon the rugh bak-fa,
We ginnled troots an bairded grunts,
Wee sookin eels an a',
Weel hud frae sicht
An frae the la.

We sa the tittle hunt the gowk
Low ower the rashy flow,
An fun the greetin peeweeps' burds
Hud on the grevel knowe,
Whar whutrets jook
An buckies grow.

We tramped laich boags an traiked stie braes,
Wae een as shairp as haks'
For ivery scroag an sit an den,
For hap-marked pads an traks;
An hurkled doon
Bae coved dake-baks.

We raked the lan frae en tae yin,
We scunged baith day an nicht;
An gien nae thocht (it's aye the wie)
Tae whut wuz wrang or richt,
Nae thocht ava.
(But noo we micht.)

But thon's a' by an lang awa –
Whut guid tae seech or sab?
Ye wait, awar the rinnin's ower,
Quait-coorached bac the hab.
Nae rinnin noo.
Nae mair. (Nae Bab.)

The sallies, hoovin saft an grey, come getherin, cloodin in.

Dailygan

by James Fenton
ORIGINALLY PUBLISHED IN ULLANS NUMMER 7, WUNTER 1999

An noo the lichts ower Brochanor
    mak blak the brae behin;
The sallies, hoovin saft an grey,
    come getherin, cloodin in;
The watter, glancin ower its dark,
    babs lippin, whusperin by;
The boag's dark sweelin, quait, aroon
    the tummock whar A lie.

The peats' quait low, the week's saft licht
    mak blak the ootby noo;
The prootas plowt; the neeps' sweet steam
    cloods roon hir sweetin broo;
Bae qua an boag, ower queelrod wa,
    thon licht's a gleekin ee
Frae whar A come an whar A'll gae
    tae nether stic nor lee.

Hae ye oany deuks, Dauvit Hugh?

Ma Graunda aun Dauvit Hugh's Deuks

by John M'Gimpsey Johnston
ORIGINALLY PUBLISHED IN ULLANS NUMMER 8, HAIRST 2001

Ma Graunfaither Jonny McGimpsey, haud twa sins, Wullum James aun Rabert John, bit baith o thum cleart aff tae America whun thae wur anly habilty hoys aun neather o thum has cum bak yit.

A mine o ma Mither sayin that Rabert John haud sade en yin o tha letters he yaest tae write tae hir noo aun then tae let hir ken hoo thae wur gettin oan, thaut baith o thum haud gaut jabs warkin aut tha coarn hervest aun jist slep unther tha threshin mill aut nicht.

Acurse, efter tha boyes tuck aff, ma Graunda wus left hes lane tae dae aa tha wark oan tha ferm. Betimes he cudnae haunnel aa tha wark hesel sae yaest tae sen fer a terble guid warker he kent tae gie him a haun. This boye wus caad Dauvit Hugh Kor.

Noo Dauvit Hugh wus a guid warker aricht bit he wus a terble quate saul aun gettin a wurd er twa oot o him wus lak puin teeth. Anly he haud nane o thum ether. Thaut wus aricht tae et cum tae mael times then Jonny ma Graunda liket a bit o a crack wac hes maet.

Sae yin nicht whun thae wur sittin aut thur supper, Jonny says tae Dauvit Hugh, bi wye o gettin a bit o a crack gaun,

'Hae ye oany deuks, Dauvit Hugh?'

Bit jist aut thaut time Dauvit Hugh wus busy peelin a pirta sae thur wus nae aunser fir a mint er twa tae Dauvit Hugh gaut tha pirta sortit. Thun he says,

'Aye'.

Jonny wusnae muckle tha wiser, sae he says tae Dauvit Hugh,

'Ir thae aa layin Dauvit Hugh?'

Ye'll notice thaut Dauvit Hugh aye gaut hes title. Oanywye, efter a bit o consuderation he says tae Jonny,

'Aye'.

Whun Jonny heert aboot aa tha deuks layin he thocht tae hesel thaut he micht bi able tae bie a wheen o Dauvit Hugh's deuk eggs acause he aye laket yin fer hes brekfaust. Sae he says tae Dauvit Hugh,

'Hoo mony hae ye Dauvit Hugh?'

Agane thur wus quate fer a while aun Jonny thocht tae hesel he's coontin thum noo, aun he amaist fell aff hes sate whun Dauvit Hugh announct proodly,

'Jist yin'.

Sae Jonny gaut nae deuk eggs fer hes brekfaust!

It wus young tae be a wain nae mair, an hard tae be a man.

Niver Loass Hairt

by Charlie Gillen
ORIGINALLY PUBLISHED IN ULLANS NUMMER 8, HAIRST 2001

Mae fether dee't whun I wus ten, I dinnae unnerstan',
It wus young tae be a wain nae mair, an hard tae be a man
I dinnae know hoo much I loast, I mebbae dinnae still,
But life for me for mony years, gane steady doon the hill.

Fae mad tae sane a wheen o' years a totter't on the brink,
At fifteen years I got a job an' loast maesel tae drink,
Aw! naw nae social drinker me, I hid maesel away
An in the courage drink afford't I got by day by day.

Sae I drunk tae dull mae senses, an I drunk tae bring me roon,
An' whut I coodnae see aff coorse, it wus maesel that I lut doon,
An whuniver I wus drunk eneuch, I cud nether see nor feel
An whuniver I wus sober, the wurl wus hard an real.

I feel't the hale thing closin' in I had loast anither fight
My wurl wus lake a tunnel but at the en' there wus nae light,
Then yin nicht as I lay stupid drunk, bereft o' even hope,
Naw a threed tae cling tae as al' aroon I grope't.

Some'dy caught mae slidin' as I near't the gates o' hell,
I think it wus mae fether, but I coodnae really tell,
That vision shuk mae, waken't me an tuk me by the han,
'Come on an mak mae proud o' ye, come on an be a man'.

Fae that tae this I tried mae best, aye, mony times I slipp't,
But that erm that led mae bak tae life, wud catch mae whun I tripp't,
An' I someway know whun I go wrang, he'll be there tae put mae richt
An if I'm in the tunnel noo, at the en' o't is a licht.

Sae I write mae rhymes o' ouler times, whun he left mae here at ten,
An whiles I think mae fether is steerin' thon oul pen,
An whether I mak ye lach or greet, I want tae mak ye think,
That some'dy oot there loves ye, nae odds hoo low ye sink.

He then wunnered if it was ony o' the gun club that toul the Polis.

The Oul Wye

by Ernest McA Scott
ORIGINALLY PUBLISHED IN ULLANS NUMMER 3, SPRING 1995

Ahoul ye A'll gie ye a spiel that'll maybe draw a lauch oot o' ye. It consarns oul Willy M'Kenzie wae a bit o' grun at the fit o' the hill whare he his fifty acre o' brave grun but thee hunner o' oul scrub on the hill. Hisell an the weechil that's quat the scholarin, young Wully, maks this new fangled silage in a big hoose that he got siller fae the Ministry tae pit up. Noo Wully was nae great shakes at this new Environment stuff an just dug a sheugh fae the pit tae the neardest burn an piped it sae nabody wud ken it was there tae tak a' the oul slurry awaw fae the pit.

Noo Wully lets oot the hill ivery year tae the nearby gun club fer rugh shootin an the club meets aboot fower times ivery wunter an spring. Noo it jest cam aboot that the twa Wullys wur pittin in silage o' the first cut an the sheugh blocked up wae tartles o' oul gress an young Wully apened it up in twa places an left them apen. It so happened that yin Setterday the Gun Club come tae shoot the hill an as luk wud hae it the Inspector o' Polis was wi them fae the nearby Berreks an had tae wak doon by the apened sheugh. Oul Wully kent fine weel the Inspector wud ken whit was gaun on an richt enough Wully got a summons tae appear at the Petty Sessions in the toon an was docked twenty-five pun for pollutin a raver. Wully pied up his twenty-five pun at the Coort an cum hame. In aboot a week's time the Inspector driv intae Wully's yerd in his ain ker an got oot.

He spoke very civil tae Wully an toul him that although he prosecuted Wully at Coort it wasnae him that clypted on him as he decided tae turn a blin' ee tae the effluent as Wully was wile good at lettin them park in his yerd whun there was a shoot, an the Inspector was gey fand o a shot. But Wully toul him richt awa that he knowed it wasnae him that clypted an this sot the Inspector a bit abak.

He then wunnered if it was ony o' the gun club that toul the Polis but Wully spoke up richt awa.

Sez Wully, 'A thocht ye micht clype on me an A got wee Sammy M'Dowell tae come up tae see me an A toul him tae ring the DOE an tell them he had information whare a burn was bein polluted but that he wanted pied for this information an A toul him tae houl oot for fifty pun. Weel he got the fifty pun, an A got the Summons an he gied me twunty-five an kep twunty-five tae hisell an A pied the fine'.

Wae that the Inspector lot oot a big trevelly o' a lauch an sez, 'I shall dine out on this one for many a long day' an wae that he sot aff fur his car wae his shouthers gaen ap an doon an driv aff.

Oul Wully loot oot a snort and hefted a lang tailed shovel oer his shouther an wint doon the loanen tae fill up the sheugh.

Hiv ye ivir smelt tha reek o a buck-goát?

A Reekin Buck-Goát, a Ringle E'ed Doag and a Wheepin Whitrick

by Isobel McCulloch
ORIGINALLY PUBLISHED IN ULLANS NUMMER 5, SIMMER 1997

Weans theday wud gie ye an oul-fashioned luk, gif ye taaked o waakin til schule – the wudnae waak tha lenth o theirsels so the wudnae. Forouten ween, times haes changed, hae – for a motèr-caur was a raie sicht in ma young day – deed thar wurnae sac monie bikes aboot ether. Weans wus mebbe mair siccar on tha roads bot.

In thaim days schule wusnae tha same as noo. Tha cane wus a quare 'deterrent' whiles (mine ye, we cudnae a toul ye whit a 'deterrent' wus gif we met yin in wur supper) – yinst ye had tha cane ye didnae want it agane. Tha wee fellas wud hae bin reddy fur it bot, for the aye kep horse-hair in thair pockets tae pit owre thair hauns – A doot it didnae work aa that weel ava. Mine ye, tha wee fellas wus verie 'gallant' bot. The wurnae allood tae cum intil tha lassies' playgrun ye see. In oor schule the did bot, for me an anither wee cuttie wus brave an guid at tha fitba an tha weefellas had need o us. When tha wee fellas wur catched the aye got a canin' bot – an tha teacher nivir laid haans on us! ('Sexual discrimination' noo!)

We didnae nyirm bot for we kent we wur weel aff. Oor teacher wus coortin ye see – she wus goin wi this fella an her heid wus fu o wee sweetie mice. Whiles we wud hae bin oot spoartin fur twa hoors an mair. We didnae ken aboot 'love' (an o coorse 'sex' hadnae bin inventit then) bot we wur nae dozers. Boys a dear we wur plaised whan we heerd tha wee moter ootside an tha teacher's face gaed pink an her een shone – we knowed we'd hae a lang playtime! We nivir let on at home bot – we wur owre cute for that – there'd a bin some ructions anent us no gittin schuled.

Dinnae be thinkin it wus aa fun bot! Heth an seng A had some near shaves waakin til tha schule an bak. A had tae waak aboot thie mile and it wus a brave step fae ma hoose til tha nixt yin. A wean cudnae dae that her lane theday, sae she cudnae. Is that whit the caa 'progress'? Ma 'hazards' wus aa o a differs bot – an lukin bak, the dinnae seem much tae git fashed owre – but hoo cum A didnae grow up wi 'complexes' aboot animals, A cudnae say! A wusnae owre feered o tha fairy thorn that wus in a fiel A had tae go by – A wud gie it a skelly aa tha same jist in case – thair wus worse things nor tha wee fowk bot.

Tha furst go-aff wus tha goát. We caa'd him a buck-goát – mebbe we shud hae caa'd him a billy-goát gif we spake Inglis. Onieroads, he wus aye waitin on me iviry morn – divil tha mind whit ye caa'd him – he knowed tha time better nor any clock. Step for step he'd waak wi me – him on tha yin side o tha dyke an me on tha tither. It wusnae much o a hedge (tha man at owned tha laun wusnae in a guid wye o daein) an thar wus slaps tha goát cud hae got thru gif he tuk tha notion – an weel A kent it. Ma hairt wud gan like tha clappers an me wunnerin whit A cud dae gif he tuk a lep thru tha slap. Hiv ye ivir smelt tha reek o a buck-goát? Gif the cud bottle it the wudnae need til use 'chemical warfare' – powerfu sae it is.

Onieroads, A'd jist got ma heid shired whan A cum til tha nixt 'hazard'. Tha furst hoose A cum til, tha road wus thair street, an tha doag wud be lyin thair waitin on me – aiblins tha goát gien him tha whud! Oh, a bad-lukin brute he wus tae an sleekit wi it – a wile ringle-e'ed divil. He wud rin at me an then jouk doon on his hunkers an folly me at ma heels – A doot he cud aisy scent ma fear. Likely that's whit he went tha hail hog fur an bit me yin morn. Man dear, bot that wus wile sair an it stertit tae beel. Ye wud harly credit it, bot the mair it was tha day tha schule nurse cum (she cum yinst or twicet a yeir tae luk for nits in tha weans' heids) A nivir toul her aboot tha bite – A nivir let on me. Did A no git tha quare tonguin for that whan A got hame – aye, an a dose o iodine on tha bites that had me leppin like a hare! A had tha mairks o thaim bites roon ma ankle for monies a lang yeir.

Tha wurst thing cum aboot jist tha yinst – yinst wus eneuch bot! Och A'd heerd tell o it like roon tha ingle at nicht whan A'd heerd aboot ghosts an banshees – ay an e'en Tam tha Divil hissel – an A'd taen it aa in tha wye weans daes. Wud ye no think A'd eneuch tae thole gangin tae schule wi'oot onie mair? Deng tha bit o it! Ah cum roon tha corner yin morn an thair it wus sut in tha middle o tha road. Mebbe it wus a whitrick, mebbe it wus a waisel. A wusnae aboot tae dae a David Attenborough on it bot. Aa A kent wus that when ye met a waisel on tha road it pit its tail in its mooth an wheeped an that brocht aa tha weasels fae aa owre tha kintra! Sae there's me, hae, staunin on tha road like a mutton-dummy, lukin at tha baste an it lukin at me – ma hairt had stapped an whan it stairtit agane it wus daein twenty til tha dizzen. A wusnae muckle mair in heecht nor twa peats an a clod, sae A hadnae daen monie yeirs on tha yird – whit A had daen flashed in front o me then bot as A waitit on tha tail tae gang in tha mooth. Whit wud come aboot efter that wis beyont me for A cud jist thole yin daeins at a time. An whan that waisel shiftit intil tha sheugh A still stud waitin tae feel ma legs agane for the had turnt til watter. Efter that A covered tha nixt mile in record time – an that lang afore Roger Bannister (him that wus tha furst boadie tae rin tha fower männit mile) wus a glint in his Da's een!

Aye tha oul fowk tuk tha haun oot o weans then – bot sure we nivir needed ony fancy psychologists wi a string o letters efter thair names tae sort oot oor complexes. Aa we daen wus tell tha same yairns tae tha yins wee'er nor us, sae as the'd be scaired forbye! Aye A mine yin day A wus cumin hame fae schule an A met tha man that belang'd tae tha goát. He had a doag wi him (no tha yin that bit me, noo) an A must hae luked a bit feerd, for he says tae me sez he, 'Dinna be afeerd lassie – tha last weelass he et he left her shuin'.

Whiles noo A think aboot aa thaim soart o things an A hae tae smile. Daes weans theday hae sich splores, ganin tae schule in tha bak o a motèr-caur?

Tha spairk o aa tha thochts A hae.

Alba an Albania

by Philip Robinson
ORIGINALLY PUBLISHED IN ULLANS NUMMER 7, WUNTER 1999

Lake gress, a boady's while, that's a'
Or lake a flure, nae last ava
A flooch o wun an al's awa
As shane as ruz
(James Fenton: "Thonner an Thon")

Boneybefore's frae whaur A'm cum,
Ma hamely hairth wi rid breek lum.
Nae mynn A hae o fechtin drum,
        Agin tha breesht.
Na, hairts wuz larnt tae saftly thrum,
        An houl oor wheesht.

Oul-farrant nichts an stane-waa ruins,
Freats ma een catched mair nor aince.
Luxemburg! Boys! A fistlin newance,
        In waffs o soon.
Duntit breeshts wi juke-bax boomins.
        Braw nichts in toun.

Willicks hoaked frae roak an wrak.
Marlies, cheesers an fairm-hoose crack.
Mair lake The Waltons nor a boadie cud tak.
        But unco shune, hae.
Slonks an dykes lept aye wud brak,
        Winkle-picker's tae.

"Kang an Kintra" no lang in thocht.
In pews, a Kang abane wuz socht.
Elvis an Country recairts bocht,
        Nae flegs aboot.
Bricht kiltie ban'? Na, no owre ocht.
        Tha heicht, A doot.

Frae keeks syne catched o ithers warls,
No yin bit oors, nae pritta farls.
But fechtin heidyins, reekin barls,
  As yins sees iz.
Warl ill divid whaur war aye birls,
  Frae poortith riz.

Wee Fergies in a lang crouse raa,
Vintage trayctors pit on a dra,
Puein wi horses gien iz mair gra,
  Fur days lang syne.
Kosovo trayctors tha yin nicht A sa,
  Oul-tyme in line.

Ticht wee Serbs, tha peep-o-day clan.
Mooslim dissenters, black-moothed an thran.
Papish Croatians bigged thair ain laun,
  "Thirteen an Echtie-Nine".
Weemin girnin owre deid guidman,
  Wrangs aye in mynn.

Waas a-tummlin gart turn ilk heid
Weans flittin, in scunners, an brithers deid
Grannie hapt in a barra, alang wi tha breid
  Nae catter ava.
Da, stour tae stour. Nae succeedin leid?
  Haud on tae Allah.

O God o Balkans, by whase haun,
Is mate gien til sic thrangs o thran?
Thrie warls, thrie leids, in yin wee lann,
      Thrie gods or Yin?
Wha cud crusade agin whilk ban',
      Whan on tha rin?

"Bal'albana's whaur A cum fae",
Tha very thing A heerd him say,
This ethnic haun o Larne yin day,
      (Whaur A wuz boarn).
Blinnin tha slonks on ilka brae.
      Hairt o Alban coarn.

A thocht A seen him yinst agane,
Thon wee auld man frae bak abane,
Hirplin Kosovo braes his lane,
      Tha gate tae bield.
Hiein frae his hairth an hame,
      Wi heirskip skailed.

Yit Boneybefore's whaur A cum frae,
Tha spairk o aa tha thochts A hae.
Whan aa bes owre, wha wudnae spae,
      Micht's aye tha thing.
Sae historie taks nae tent theday,
      O a weefella's spring.

Ivery apprentice has to make the tea.

The Wee Bleck Can

by Hugh Robinson
ORIGINALLY PUBLISHED IN ULLANS NUMMER 6, SPRING 1998

[Editors' note: This story is part of the author's collection of short stories, Across the Fields of Yesterday, published in 1999 by Ullans Press, Belfast.]

Schuil-days, the happiest days o ma life, shuin cam tae an enn. As Ah hae sayed afore, Ah feenished ma days o formal education at Newton Tech - the oul Tech - in Sooth Street. But Ah wus fifteen noo, an Ah cudnae get left schuil quick eneuch. Tae get awa fae it Ah tuk a joab in Walker's Flax Mill whuch rin alangside the canal bank in the toon.

Ah niver liked the mill. Ah waanted tae be a cairpenter. Ah wus right an skeely wi ma hauns an Ah liked warkin wi wud. A cairpenter. Thon's whut Ah waanted tae be.

Weel, Ah hud a bit o guid luck. Twa-three months efter Ah stairted in the mill, in the month o May, Ah seen an advertisement in the *Spectator*:

> Wanted. Young man, age 15-16, to serve apprenticeship in
> joinery trade. Apply at once in person to: W J Orr, 6a Albert
> Street, Bangor.

Thon wus jist the chance Ah wus lukkin fer, an Ah determined the joab wud be mine. The very nixt moarnin, at hauf-past seeven, Ah wus oan ma bike, an ridin the sax mile owre tae Bangor. Ah maun hae made a guid eneuch impression oan Mr Orr. Ah goat the joab.

Noo, there's mony a yairn Ah cud come aff wi aboot ma days in the biggin trade, an maybe Ah'll dae that, in anither book. But fer noo, Ah waant tae tell ye aboot ma first encoonter wi ma new warkmates, an the wee bleck can.

It wus ma joab tae mak the tay. That's whut Woodbine sayed. Ah wusnae convinced. Ah gawked in unco confusion as ma new mates gaithert aroon me in the front room o the wee hoose we wur gan tae renovate in a Belfast bek street, jist aff the Albertbrig Road. Aa trades wur representit there: painters, plumbers, jiners, plaisterers, brickies an spairks, an each an ivery yin o them wus houlin oot tae me his very ain bleck an battered billy-can, an a wee tin container wi yin enn mairked 'sugar' an the ither enn mairked 'tea'.

'Ivery apprentice has to make the tea when he starts in the buildin trade', Woodbine informed me. 'So it's your job to do it'.

Ah still wusnae convinced. Ah gawked at Woodbine, a wee fat fella wi a flair-brush moustache an a baldy heid. Ah gawked at the jummle o billy-cans an the expectant expression oan the faces o their owners.

Ah jist cudnae unnerstaun this. Ah kenned it wus ma first day oan the joab, an aa that. But Ah wus the new apprentice jiner. Ah hud ma ain hammer an screw-driver an Ah wus savin up fer a saw. Ah shud be makkin dove-tail joints an hingin dures an biggin stair-cases. Ah wus a tradesman. No a tay-wetter. A fella in ma position hud tae mak a bit o a staun.

'Ah dinnae ken hoo tae dae it', Ah declared, hopin this wud throw the billy-can houlers aff the scent. It wus proabably the warst thing Ah cud hae sayed.

'We know you don't know how to do it', giggled Woodbine. 'That's what ye're here for. To learn. Come on. I'll show you'.

The effect o Woodbine's statement wus simthin akin tae the apenin o the grey-houn traps at Dunmore oan a Friday nicht. Ivery man in the place as hud a billy-can wus oan tap o me in a flash, pilin them intae ma airms an addin the wee containers o tay an shuggar, as weel as paper pokes at Ah shuin fun oot helt a mäxture o baith, blended wi care tae suit the palate o its owner.

Ah staggered unnerneath the jummle an tried tae mak sense o the guldert oarders as tae whuther the tay wus tae be made strang or wake an hoo mich or hoo little shuggar wus tae be added, an tae whut level the cans wus tae be filled. Ah clung desperately tae the tins an cans an peckets, wunnerin hoo Ah wud iver min wha belanged tae whuch, let alane whit his parteeklar gastronomical preference micht be.

'Have you got a can of your own?' queried Woodbine oan the road oot tae the bek yaird.

Ah shuk ma heid fae ahin the moontain o cans as Ah tripped owre a hauf beg o cement lyin at the bek dure. Ah'd niver seen a billy-can tae twa meenits syne. Ah didnae ken it wus pairt o a jiner's gear.

'Niver mind', grinned Woodbine. 'I'll lend ye my oul one'. He pointed tae a watter-tap hingin loose fae the white-waashed waa in the yaird. 'Fill them cans an bring them over here an' I'll show ye how to light a fire'.

Ah tuk the cans owre tae the tap an tried tae scrub the bleckness o grime fae inside the biggest yin. Woodbine seen me an wus at ma elbow in a flash. 'What do ye think ye're doin?' he bawled, grabbin the can fae me.

'Ah'm tryin tae clane it!' Ah guldert bek at him, stertin tae get a bit fed up wi the hale business o tay-makkin. 'Luk at the state o it! It's boggin!'

'Don't be daft', snorted Woodbine, giein me a cuff roon the ear. 'It takes weeks to get a can into a good black state like that. NIVER, IVER wash a billy-can! Ye just rinse them.

That black carbon on the can adds to the flavour of the tea. Niver wash a billy-can'.

Ah lifted the cans an kerried them owre tae whaur Woodbine hud stairted tae prepare a fire. He'd clodded twa or three breeks thegither tae mak a soart o a square, wi a hole in the middle. He tossed a haunfu o wud-shavins intae the hole an lukked up at me.

'First of all, we light the shavins. Okay?'

It seemed like a guid idea tae me. Ah nodded ma heid. 'Okay. We licht the shavins'.

'Okay', echoed Woodbine. 'We light the shavins'. He struck a match an drapped it oan tap o the curly white ribbons o wud.

They flared up immediately. Woodbine nodded his heid in satisfaction an winked at me as if he hud jist tuk yin giant step forrit fer mankine. He tossed a couple o cuttins o wud intae the bleeze an apened up the breeks fer better ventilation, stressin oan me the absolute necessity o daein this. Yince he hud goat the fire established he planked three iron rods, each aboot a quairter o an inch thick, acroass the tap o the breeks. Very precisely, he positioned aa the cans oan tap o the rods. Ah watched, fascinated by it aa as the flames licked hungrily roon the cans.

Syne Woodbine did a gye unco thing. He lifted a hatchet an split a wheen o pieces o wud aboot an inch lang an a quairter o an inch thick. Wi the delicacy o a concert pianist he drapped them, yin by yin, intae each o the cans.

It wusnae ony guid. Ah tried tae figger it oot. But Ah cudnae dae it.

'Why did ye pit the wud intae the cans?' sez Ah.

Woodbine smiled an nodded wisely. 'That', he med me answer, draa'in himsel up tae his fu heicht o roon aboot five fit twa inches, 'that is the most important part of the whole procedure. That wee bit of wood keeps the smoke out of the can. And don't you ever forget to put it in. Them boys'll have yer life if ye give them smoky tea'.

Ah watched the reek swirl aroon the cans whuch wur aready pitted wi the bleckness o a hunner fires. Ah wusnae aa that shair Woodbine wusnae coddin me. Ah decided tae test him.

'Woodbine', sez Ah, 'hoo daes the wud keep the reek oot?'

Woodbine shrugged. 'How do I know how it keeps it out? I'm a brickie's labourer, not Professor Einstein! But it works. So you make sure ye put it in. Right?' He paused an fummled aboot in the poacket o his dungarees. 'I don't suppose you've got a feg on ye? A Woodbine even?'

Ah gien a bit o a lauch an shuk ma heid as it dawned oan me of a suddent hoo Woodbine hud come by his nickname. 'Ah'm sorry, Woodbine', sez me. ' Ah dinnae smoke'.

Woodbine lauched an tossed his heid in the air as he stairted tae slip tay an shuggar intae the boilin cans. 'Niver mind. Ah'll pick up a wee butt somewhere …' He pu'd oot a foldin rule fae yin o his poackets an slipped it unner the haunles o the cans. Yin by yin he liftit them fae the fire an set them in a straucht line oan the grun.

'Now', he demonstrated, 'to get the tea-leaves to settle, ye jist tap the side o the cans like this'. He gien each o the cans a dunt wi the side o the rule an the tay-leaves sank magically tae the bottom. Syne he picked up a narra lathe o wud an slipped it unner the haunles o the five cans, pickin them aa up in the yin go.

Ah lifted the last twa wi a lump o wud, jist as Woodbine hud daen. Ah wus feelin richt plased wi masel. 'Whit aboot cups?' Ah axed. 'Whaur's the cups?'

Woodbine set his rail o cans oan the grun an stared at me in exasperation. 'Cups!' he repeated incredulously, lood eneuch fer hauf o Belfast tae hear. 'Cups! What wud ye be wantin cups for? Sure they'd only ruin the taste of the tea. You'll drink it straight from the can, the way any other civilized bein wud do. You won't be needin any cups!'

Woodbine moved a wee bit nearder tae me an waved a fing'r unner ma neb. 'An I'll tell ye somethin else. As long as you live, an wheriver ye go, ye'll niver drink a better drap o tea than what you'll drink from a wee black can'.

Ye ken, Ah'm gled it wus ma joab tae wet the tay thon day. An Woodbine wus richt. Ah hae wrocht oan mony a joab syne, an in mony different places. Fortune haes favoured me, an Ah hae dined wi the rich an famous, in luxury an opulence at wud be mich grander nor ma natural habitat.

But whauriver Ah hae been, an whutiver Ah hae drunk fae, Ah hae niver tastit a drap o tay as wud come onywhaur near thon sweet, strang, an wudden brew Ah first tastit aa thae years bek, fae a wee bleck can.

A' his ta'kin' wus dain in his guid aul' North Antrim Dialect o tha Ulster-Scot Leid.

Thae Tuk Mae Ain Tung

by Charlie Reynolds
ORIGINALLY PUBLISHED IN ULLANS NUMMER 8, HAIRST 2001

Mae name is Charlie Rannals (Reynolds) an A wus boarn weel owre fifty year ago in tha toonlan' o Kilmail (Kilmoyle), Benverdin, Dervock, that lies tae tha North o tha Coonty o Antrim. Oor femelie moved a' owre the parishes o North Antrim, tae at last wae upped sticks an tuk aff tae tha big toon o Coulren (Coleraine).

Noo A wus aboot six year aul' at tha time an had bain tae then blessed wae tha soun' o mae ain guid Ulster-Scot Leid as wus used bae a' mae ain yins. Lukin' bak noo A am gled tae bae able tae min' tha lake o mae granfaither takin' aboot tha peat binks, clockin' hens, tha aul' soo's an ta'kin' aboot hes work alang tha wee nerra gage relwye that run fornenst his hoose tae Bellykassle. A' his ta'kin' wus dain in his guid aul' North Antrim Dialect o tha Ulster-Scot Leid.

Hooiniver whun wae moved tae tha toon things changed for iver. A wus lached at deh an nicht aboot tha wye A ta'ked. Tha maist o tha wains at tha schuil thocht A wus a kinna o an oddity frae tha Garry boag, naw that thae micht hae kent whaur tha boag wus onywye.

Things went frae bad tae worse an owre tha years wae tha tants o mae plae-mates an tha goulin' o tha aul' teachers, thae tried tae tak mae ain tung aff mae. Even mae ain yins wha still ta'k tha aul' tung thocht it wus better that their aff-spring got redd o it in tha name o progress. Noo A'm sure thae a' meent weel enouch but it haes left mae wae mair nor a chip on mae shoother an mair nor scunnered aboot the wye oor ain tung wus tore frae iz, and o coorse tha Irish Language had a bad time as weel an wus scoarned on bae the establishment o tha deh.

A'm gled things ir at last beginnin' tae change for tha better an tha richt tae ta'k in yer ain tung is at last baein respeected. Tha mair tha wye A ta'k noo mae hae strayed a brav bit frae tha wye mae granfaither ta'ked A feel mair nor proud tae lee ahint mae some o tha Leid that is sae bonnie tae mae an is tha Leid o mae sowl. An min' ye if up in heaven thae dinnae hae a wee korner that ye kan whiles tak a danner intae an ta'k in yer aul' tung A wull bae soart o drunted